finding life on death row

Advisor in Criminal Justice to Northeastern University Press
Gilbert Geis

finding life on death row

profiles of six inmates

Katya Lezin

· · · · · · · ·

Northeastern University Press
Boston

Northeastern University Press

Library of Congress Cataloging-in-Publication Data

Lezin, Katya, 1965–
    Finding life on death row : profiles of six death
row inmates / Kaya Lezin.
        p. cm.
    ISBN 1-55553-405-8 (cloth : alk. paper)
    ISBN 1-55553-457-0 (pbk. : alk. paper)
    1. Death row inmates—United States—Case
studies. I. Title.
HV8699.U6L49   1999
364.15'23'092273—dc21
    [B]   99-31731

Designed by Janis Owens

Composed in Janson by Graphic Composition, Inc.,
Athens, Georgia. Printed and bound by Maple Press,
York, Pennsylvania. The paper is Sebago Antique, an
acid-free sheet.

MANUFACTURED IN THE UNITED STATES OF AMERICA

04   03   02   01   00   6   5   4   3

to Noah and Hannah,
in the hope that the death penalty
will no longer exist by the time they are old enough
to understand what it is.

contents

foreword

The United States is one of the few industrialized nations in the world that retains the death penalty. Today, four nations—China, Iran, Saudia Arabia, and the United States—account for 80 percent of the documented executions that occur in the world each year. In the last decade, the United States has been one of a very few countries that has executed people who were children at the time of commission of their crimes.

Thirty years ago it appeared that the United States would also abandon capital punishment. The death penalty was seldom used in the 1960s, and the U.S. Supreme Court declared it unconstitutional in 1972 because it was arbitrarily imposed. However, after the Supreme Court's decision, a number of states passed new capital punishment statutes that were upheld by the Supreme Court in 1976. Today, thirty-eight states, the federal government, and the military have laws authorizing the death penalty. Federal law authorizes the death penalty for over fifty crimes, making the death penalty available even in those states and territories that have refused to enact capital punishment statutes. Over 3,500 men, women, and children are waiting to be injected, electrocuted, gassed, shot, or hanged. The number of executions carried out has steadily increased during the 1990s. Hundreds of people have been killed by the states since the Supreme Court's decision in 1976 that allowed the resumption of capital punishment. Over 90 percent of those executions have taken place in the nation's "death belt," the states of the old Confederacy. The taking of human life by the state has become "routine."

A society that employs such an enormous, severe, irreversible, and violent penalty, which has been discarded by much of the rest of the world, should at least know whom it is killing. It should understand the process that determines who lives and who dies. The death penalty is authorized for thousands of people who commit crimes each year, but only about 275 are sentenced to death. Even fewer are actually put to death. Who are those people? How were they selected to die when so many others—some with worse histories of criminal behavior and guilty of far more heinous crimes—were punished with life imprisonment? Are those condemned to death really the worst of the worst criminals in our society? These are questions of fundamental importance for, as Supreme Court Justice William Brennan observed, "the way in which we choose those who will die reveals the depth of moral commitment among the living." But the condemned have received too little attention. And as the number of executions continues to increase, less and less attention is being paid to who is being killed and how they were condemned to die.

The first few executions after the Supreme Court upheld the resumption of capital punishment received attention locally and, in some instances, nationally. The countdown to the first execution in each state was covered attentively by the media, much like the countdown to the launch of a spacecraft. But too often attention was focused on inconsequential details, such as what the condemned person ate at his last meal, how the executioner was chosen, the posturing of politicians competing for credit for the kill, or the mechanics of execution—the firing squad in Utah, electric chairs that continually malfunctioned in Alabama and Florida, lethal gas in Mississippi and California, hanging in Washington, and the "new and improved" method of execution used by Texas and most other states—lethal injection.

These early executions were accompanied by demonstrations for and against the death penalty. On the edge of the prison grounds, nuns and a few other opponents burned candles in protest while a much larger contingent, usually led by members of college fraternities, threw beer parties in celebration. The Ku Klux Klan turned out in full regalia for some executions in Georgia. Police officers sold T-shirts with slogans like "Crank up Old Sparky" when the killer of a fellow officer was put to death in Florida. Some people even brought their children to be a part of it all. The media covered and often contributed to the carnival atmosphere surrounding executions.

As unseemly as much of this activity was, it nevertheless alerted the public to the fact that someone was being killed in its name. Usually, the public was informed about the crime committed and the harm done to the community and the victim's family and friends. The public seldom learned about the person executed and the process that led to his or her condemnation. There were and continue to be exceptions, however, such as the serial killers Theodore Bundy and John Wayne Gacy, the born-again Christian Carla Faye Tucker, and Jerome Bowden, a mentally retarded youth whose execution in 1986 prompted such outrage that Georgia passed a law prohibiting execution of the mentally retarded. But in most instances, the condemned remained largely anonymous, defined only by the worst thing they have ever done.

Today most executions go unnoticed even in the communities and states where they are carried out. They receive little, if any, coverage in the media, and only a handful of people, if anyone, show up to protest or support executions. Politicians assure us that by executing people we are demonstrating our moral outrage and are showing that we are tough on crime. We are told that that those we are killing are not human. They are "animals." They are "predators"—some children are even described as "superpredators." As in a war against another nation, the proponents of the war on crime describe the enemy as a faceless group so evil and so lacking in humanity, feelings, and worth that their elimination is justified.

But as in all wars, the casualties of the war on crime are human. And as in all wars, there are innocent victims. Over seventy people condemned to die have been released in the last twenty years after their innocence was clearly established. Others have had their death sentences commuted to life imprisonment without the possibility of parole because of doubts about their guilt, and some have been executed despite questions of innocence. U.S. Representative Bill McCollum of Florida has stated that the risk of executing the innocent must be accepted if we are to have capital punishment. Once we were taught that it is better that some guilty people go free than an innocent person be convicted. Today, we are told that innocent people who are wrongfully executed are acceptable casualties in the war on crime.

But even those who have offended society most grievously by committing murder are human. They have mothers, fathers, children, spouses, and friends. Like all humans, they are neither all good nor all bad. But they are much more than the worst thing they ever did. Many of those condemned to die faced enormous disadvantages from birth, such as denial of education, opportunity, and hope because of their race, debilitating poverty, abuse, neglect, mental illness, mental retardation, and lack of maturity and judgment. None of these considerations excuses or justifies the terrible crimes they may have committed. But they raise important questions, such as whether those condemned to die are so far beyond redemption that they should be eliminated from the human community, and whether the death penalty is being imposed on the worst criminals or on the poorest and most powerless members of society. A youth from a dysfunctional family with mental limitations who panicked and killed someone in a botched attempt to rob a convenience store is arguably less culpable, and thus less deserving of death, than, say, the executive of a tobacco company who with full knowledge of the consequences of his actions continued year after year to push an addictive lethal product on millions of people, covering up evidence of its dangers, misleading the public, and spending millions of dollars to hook children on it.

In the pages that follow, Katya Lezin goes behind the slogans and sound bites of the war on crime to help answer these questions. She describes six people condemned to die by the states of Alabama, Georgia, and South Carolina. She tells about their crimes, their cases, their lives, and the agony and torment endured by their families. She describes whom society is killing, how it was determined that they would die, and how state and federal courts responded to challenges to their convictions and sentences. Two of those she describes have been executed. One is no longer in prison, released in 1993 and now married and a useful and productive member of society. The remaining three are no longer under death sentences, but they are serving terms of life imprisonment.

Joseph Carl Shaw, a military policeman who suffered from schizophrenia, was medicating himself with illegal drugs after the disintegration of his marriage. After begging for help and being turned away from a military mental health clinic, he committed two murders. Shaw had never been in trouble with the law before. His parents—hard-working, middle-class residents of Kentucky—received a telephone call informing them that their son was charged with murder and faced the death penalty in South Carolina. A court-appointed lawyer advised Shaw to plead guilty and put his fate in the hands of a single person, a politically ambitious judge who had served in the state legislature and hoped for a seat he ultimately obtained on the South Carolina Supreme Court. Shaw followed the lawyer's advice.

Donald Wayne Thomas also suffered from schizophrenia and struggled through childhood with the violence and chaos arising from the alcoholism of his mother and her friends. He may very well have been innocent of the crime for which he was condemned to die by a Georgia jury, but the single lawyer assigned to defend him failed to investigate the facts. After finding him guilty of the crime, the jury that was called upon to decide if he should live or die was not told one word about his mental illness or his family background. Many years later, when a new legal team of volunteer lawyers took over Thomas's case, the trail was so cold and Thomas's disability was so great that it was impossible to sort out whether Thomas was guilty or innocent.

Michael Cervi, the son of a California homicide detective, left the U.S. Navy ship on which he was stationed and robbed and murdered a doctor who had picked up Cervi and a companion while they were hitchhiking across the country. He was sentenced to death in a small rural county in Georgia. His family had the means to hire a competent attorney, but they were powerless to prevent the local prosecutor from engaging in repeated acts of misconduct during the trial.

Judy Haney, convicted of killing a man who had abused her and her children for fifteen years, was represented at her capital trial in Talladega, Alabama, by a lawyer who appeared in court so drunk that the judge had to suspend the trial for a day and send him to jail to dry out. The next day both lawyer and client were produced from jail, and the trial resumed. Jerry Fielding, the elected state court judge who presided over Haney's case, was so unconcerned about the lawyer's intoxication and justice for Haney that he appointed him to handle her appeal.

Jimmy Horton, an African American, was sentenced to death by an all-white jury in Macon, Georgia. Horton and Pless Brown were in the process of burglarizing an unoccupied apartment when the resident returned home. She was accompanied by a man who obtained a gun and confronted the burglars as they attempted to flee through the back door of the apartment. Shots were fired, and the man was killed. He was Macon's elected prosecutor, the district attorney.

It was never determined which burglar fired the fatal shot. But the racial composition of the jury determined which burglar was sentenced to die. At Horton's trial, prosecutor Joe Briley, as was his habit, used his discretionary jury strikes to eliminate all black citizens from the jury. Horton, represented by court-appointed lawyers who distanced themselves from him and offered only the most perfunctory defense, was sentenced to death. Brown, who was also African American, was more fortunate. He was tried before a jury that included five members of his race. He received a life sentence.

Larry Gene Heath, sentenced to death for the kidnapping and murder of his pregnant wife, was represented by a court-appointed lawyer so indifferent to his fate that on an appeal of Heath's case, the lawyer filed a brief before the Alabama Supreme Court that contained only a single page of argument. The lawyer did not even appear before the court at his only opportunity to present an oral argument.

We live in a time of sound bites and cynicism. But life is more complicated and more hopeful. The politicians who compete to show who is the toughest on crime say that those who commit crimes are cold, uncaring, without remorse, and totally beyond redemption and any prospect for rehabilitation. But we learn in one chapter that someone who committed a cold, carefully planned, and extraordinarily vile murder later became an ordained minister and such a positive force in prison that even the Alabama commissioner of corrections cried at his execution. We learn of another, sentenced to die as a youth, who was released on parole after his death sentence was overturned.

Five of the six individuals described in this book, like almost all of those sentenced to death, were poor and thus unable to afford a lawyer to defend them. They were represented by lawyers assigned to them, usually by the presiding judge, at their trials and their first appeals. Their lawyers were paid only token amounts to defend complex cases involving life and death. And in each case, the system got what it paid for: perfunctory representation from lawyers not fully aware of the procedures and legal issues involved in a capital trial, lawyers who lacked the time and resources to investigate the cases adequately or consult with experts. But it was Joseph Shaw, Donnie Thomas, Judy Haney, Jimmy Horton, and Larry Heath who suffered the consequences of the system's stinginess. Only Michael Cervi, whose family could afford to hire a lawyer, was represented by a caring and capable individual.

In later stages of review of their cases, called "post-conviction review," or habeas corpus, those too poor to hire a lawyer are completely dependent upon attorneys who volunteer their services to them free of charge. Four of the six individuals described in this book were successful in avoiding execution at these later stages, which shows how important these stages are. Nevertheless, the U.S. Supreme Court has held that no one has a right to a court-appointed lawyer for these critical appeals to the courts of last resort.

As a consequence, many of those facing the death penalty in the United States have no lawyer at all for these stages of review. Some are forced to represent themselves, even in capital cases. But even the death row inmate who has the good fortune to receive the services of a competent lawyer willing to work for free soon finds that the lawyer is limited by the way the case was handled by the lawyers assigned to defend the case at trial. For example, the failure of the appointed lawyer to make an objection, which may be the result of ignorance of the law, or the lawyer's failure to present evidence, perhaps because he or she does not realize its importance or lacks the resources to find witnesses and bring them to court, will prevent a reviewing court from examining those issues later on.

In these six cases, judges sworn to uphold the Constitution of the United States display a remarkable indifference to injustice, which is typical of the process by which people are condemned to die. Fairness has become the ultimate casualty of the war on crime. State court judges are popularly elected in Alabama and Georgia and are chosen by the legislature in South Carolina. They are highly political and cannot afford to appear "soft on crime" if they wish to remain in office or advance to a higher one.

A South Carolina trial court judge with ambitions of being on the state supreme court, which he later realized, was warned that unless he sentenced Joseph Carl Shaw to death he would be "holding court in Walhalla for the rest of his life." Judge Alex Crumley gave lawyers thirty days to brief the issues in Donald Thomas's case, but then issued his ruling against Thomas before receiving the brief. Judge Jerry Fielding presided over a case in which the defense lawyer was too intoxicated to represent the client. Instead of initiating proceedings to disbar the attorney, Judge Fielding appointed him to handle the appeal. (The lawyer failed to submit a brief on time and lawyers from the Southern Center for Human Rights handled the appeal.)

In Larry Heath's case, the Alabama Supreme Court accepted a one-page brief that would not have received a passing grade in a first-year legal writing class at any law school in the United States. The lawyer did not show up for oral argument. If the court, faced with the momentous task of reviewing a capital case, had been concerned about justice, it would have appointed a competent lawyer to write a brief and argue the case. But the Alabama Supreme Court simply affirmed the conviction and death sentence on the basis of the one page submitted to it.

Review of capital cases by federal judges has often resulted in the correction of injustices ignored by the state courts, including some of those described in this book. Federal judges are appointed for life. While the appointment of federal judges is very political, once they are on the bench, federal judges are more insulated from day-to-day political pressure than state court judges. But recently Congress severely restricted the power of federal courts to review state court convictions. It also eliminated funding for some important programs established in the mid-1980s. These programs found volunteer lawyers to represent the condemned in later stages of review and advised those lawyers on how to handle cases. The programs also provided representation to many of the condemned. The elimination of funding for the programs has left many people under death sentences without lawyers to represent them during critical stages of review.

As a result of these developments, there will be less review of death sentences by courts, and more executions in the future. Some of the individuals described in this book who are no longer under death sentences would not have had their death sentences set aside under the more restrictive laws now in existence. They would have been executed. That makes this book all the more important. Society should not be indifferent to such a momentous act as the killing of a human being by the state, no matter how frequently those acts occur.

Society should ask whether those condemned to die are a subhuman species so evil, cold, and remorseless that execution is the only just response to their crimes. Or could anyone, like the parents of Joseph Carl Shaw, receive a telephone call relating that a son or daughter, afflicted by mental illness and influenced by drugs, had committed unspeakable acts and faces the death penalty? Could anyone find herself in the position of Judy Haney, trapped in an abusive relationship, and so impaired in her judgment that killing appears to be the only way out? Can we even begin to imagine how it feels to be constantly tormented by voices, fears, and other manifestations of schizophrenia? Can we say with regard to any of the six people described in this book, there but for the grace of God go I?

This book will help those struggling with the moral and practical questions raised by the death penalty. No book can address all of those questions, but this one will help the reader decide whether there is something about those condemned to die or about the crimes they committed that requires their elimination from the human community, or whether they are in fact our children, our brothers, our sisters, our neighbors, and members of our community, who, despite the enormity of their crimes, can be punished for their transgressions in less drastic, less degrading, and less violent ways that recognize their humanity, their frailties, and the possibility of atonement and redemption.

Stephen B. Bright

I am adamantly opposed to the death penalty for several reasons, any one of which, in my mind, justifies its abolition. It is well documented that the death penalty has no deterrent value, so its only purpose is that of revenge and punishment. As such, it puts the United States in some pretty poor company—countries whom we as a nation routinely cite for human rights violations. An execution involves ending the life of an individual, often making us guilty of the very crime for which we are punishing someone. It also discounts any belief in redemption and forgiveness, reflecting a short-sighted and dismal view of humanity. And our flawed criminal justice system does not guarantee that those convicted and sentenced were fully protected and represented as required by our Constitution. In fact, the possibility exists that we will convict and execute an innocent person.

My hope, however, is that those of you who do not share my views will read this book. It is not about six individuals who are totally innocent and wrongly convicted, nor is it about those who committed crimes undeserving of punishment. In fact, I intentionally selected a variety of individuals who admit, to varying degrees, to committing the crimes for which they are charged. All of the crimes described in this book involve ending a life, and some of them are horrible, depraved acts. In several instances, when I read the case law and the descriptions of the crimes these defendants committed, I felt an overwhelming sense of disgust and anger. I wanted to punish the defendants and hurt them in much the same way they had inflicted pain and suffering on others. But when I began to dig a little deeper into their legal and personal histories and learned about them as individuals, the horror of what they had done was matched by shame and sympathy for what they had endured.

Another common thread of the cases presented in this book is the abysmal legal representation many of the individuals initially received. I hope that even staunch supporters of the death penalty will appreciate the inequity of our current system. Punishments today are far more a function of the quality of the defendant's legal representation than the crime he or she committed.

My intent in profiling these individuals and telling their stories is not to excuse their crimes, but to present the crimes in the context of their entire lives. I readily admit to trying to humanize individuals who are traditionally reduced to stark numbers and sensationalized facts. As Stephen Bright often says, "We are more than the worst thing we have ever done."

acknowledgments

To say Stephen Bright gave this book his blessing would be to understate the extent of his support. From his unequivocal enthusiasm when I first approached him with the idea, to his assistance with all aspects of researching and writing it, he literally made this book happen. His dedication and selfless commitment to defending those who most need counsel and to improving our legal system are truly inspiring. It has been an honor working with him.

Equally inspiring are the efforts of the other attorneys and prison administrators featured in this book. I appreciate their generosity with respect to their files, memories, and time, and I applaud the work that they do.

I would also like to thank the individuals who graciously agreed to be profiled in this book, as well as their families. I know the experiences they recollected and shared were painful, and I feel honored to be the one to document them. I hope this book does justice to their lives.

It would be impossible to list everyone who supported me in this endeavor. I therefore thank all my friends, colleagues, and family who provided encouragement throughout the writing of this book. Despite the inevitable risk of oversight, I would like to single out the following individuals for their insight, editing, and overall support: Jessica Brown, Jim Crawford, Lauren Dubin, Debra King, Jessi Morrison, Nancy Ruso, Beth Sherman, Thierry Van Bastaeler, Abbie Willard, and Kristen Zarenko.

At the risk of writing a separate book consisting solely of acknowledgments, I would like to mention a few more people deserving of special recognition. My parents, Arthur and Alice Lezin, encouraged not only the writing of this book but all of my efforts and pursuits throughout my life. Their support and guidance, not to mention their own accomplishments and commitment to public interest, are largely responsible for who I am today. My in-laws, Norman and Susanne Lieberman, provided child care on numerous occasions, allowing me to complete what two toddlers would have otherwise rendered an impossible feat. My dear friend Laurie Wahlig is a constant cheerleader for all that I do; her enthusiasm means a lot. My sister, Nicole Lezin, went above and beyond the call of duty. She opened her home in Atlanta to me during my many research trips and offered transportation and company for several prison visits. She also provided invaluable editing on what I optimistically thought were final drafts of the chapters. Her support—both monetary and emotional—was phenomenally generous and appreciated.

Lastly, I would like to thank my husband, David. I hereby award him the "Supportive Spouse Medal of Honor" for his encouragement and generosity throughout the writing of this book. Much of the credit for my success in juggling my many roles and responsibilities belongs to him.

j.c. shaw

Dear Karyn,

 It was about 4:30 when I pulled into the drive way. You were in the back yard wearing a halter top and cut off blue geans. In the back yard was a swing set and a sand box. The grass was green and the yard was fenced in. When I opened the gate, Jennifer, our little girl came running to me and said your home daddy. I picked her up and gave her a kiss and said yes I'm home. I then walked over to you and kissed you. You asked me how my day was and I said fine. I had a present for Jennifer because it was her birthday. When we got into the house she ran to get her report card. It had all A's and B's on it. I told her that she had done very good in school. You had cooked a meat loaf for supper. After supper the cake and ice-cream was brought out. It has 7 candels on it. After we ate the cake and ice-cream she opened her presents. It was a yellow dress with yellow ribbons for her pony tail. She had a great big smile on her face and said thankyou to you and me. It was now about 9:30. We looked at each other and said it was time to go to bed for ourselves. We turned all the lights off except for the bathroom light in case Jennifer woke up in the middle of the night. We sat in bed for about 15 minutes and talked about how lucky we were to have a daughter like her. I reached over to give you a hug and a kiss, but before I could kiss you the guy next to me woke me up and said it was time for chow. I hope part of this dream comes true for you Karyn because I know now it will never happen to me because now I am in Jail for killing 3 people. I'll probably be dead in a year because they want to give me the death penalty, so I hope you can find a life like the one I wrote about Karyn.

Love,
J.C.

 J.C. Shaw married Karyn Negrich, his high school sweetheart, on March 31, 1973. It was his eighteenth birthday. Their wedding photo shows a young white man with abundant dark hair, long sideburns, and a thick mustache. His large hands hang at the sides of his six-foot-three-inch frame as if he doesn't know what to do with them, and he has the slightest hint of a smile on his face. His bride, looking much more like her eighteen years, is beaming. The proud parents flank the newlyweds on both sides, all clearly happy with the match.

 Following the wedding, J.C. moved from the house he shared with his mother, stepfather, and three half-brothers to his in-laws' home. He and Karyn were happy on the Gibson farm. J.C. helped Karyn's father and grandfather with the farm work, and the young couple often babysat Karyn's little brother, Tim.

Babysitting younger brothers was not new to J.C. He was eight when Robert Jr., the first of his three half-brothers, was born. Robert Jr. was followed by Dennis three years later, and by Gregory one year after Dennis. Since both parents worked outside the home, J.C. helped raise his younger brothers, often caring for them in his parents' absence. All three boys looked up to J.C. and loved him, but Robert Jr. revered him most. He and J.C. shared a room, and Robert Jr. spent most of his free time shadowing his big brother. He tagged along to J.C.'s basketball games and later, when J.C. bought his first car with money he'd borrowed from his parents, Robert Jr. hitched rides with J.C. to his own basketball games. He still remembers the ride back from the game in which he scored a basket for the opposing team. Completely devastated, Robert Jr. was convinced he could never show his face again, but J.C. was able to tease him and console him in a way that no one else could.

J.C. was a generous and involved older brother. He coached Robert Jr.'s Little League team and even let Robert accompany him and Karyn on a double date, despite the eight-year age difference between them. J.C. spent hours wrestling with his brothers down in the basement, and always referred to them as "the kids." Even when Robert Jr., Dennis, and Greg were out of high school, J.C. continued to call them "the kids." One Christmas, his parents told him he would not be getting much that year because money was tight. "Don't worry," J.C. responded. "Just buy for the kids."

Joseph Carl Shaw was born on March 31, 1955, to Melvin and Mary Shaw in Louisville, Kentucky. By the time he was three, his parents were divorced. The following year, his mother married Robert Crum, her second husband. J.C.'s father maintained some contact with him until his eighth birthday, but abandoned him after that. J.C. was a happy child, but very fidgety and hyperactive. Drugs were prescribed early on to calm him down. He also suffered from sudden high temperatures, some as high as 107 degrees, which sent him into convulsions.

Over six feet tall by the time he was thirteen years old, J.C. was the tallest and largest boy in his class. His height served him well in sports, which he pursued much more enthusiastically and successfully than his school work. He was one of the better players in the Catholic basketball league for the city of Louisville, and he also excelled on the football field. At school, though, J.C. struggled to get C's. After flunking a grade, J.C. eventually dropped out of high school. He had completed the tenth grade. "For some reason," he later explained, "I just didn't get along with school work. School for me just didn't work out. I don't know why."

His first job after leaving school was as a bag boy at a local supermarket. Within a short while, however, J.C. joined his stepfather finishing drywall. He was a hard worker and a good "wipe down" man; he and Robert Sr. enjoyed working together. He also enjoyed playing practical jokes on his stepfather, who often fell for J.C.'s pranks. Once J.C. called and pretended to be a homeowner wanting a quote on how much it would cost to paint his house. Robert Sr. made it through several rounds of questions before realizing that it was J.C. Later, when J.C. was in the Army, he would call from the corner store but pretend that he was still in South Carolina.

Despite growing up during a time when rebellion was the norm, J.C. was respectful and loving toward his parents. He stuck to his 11:00 P.M. curfew (even though Karyn, whom he was dating at the time, had a 1:00 A.M. curfew), kept his room neat, and willingly watched "the kids" each day until his parents returned home from work. The only time he ever asked his parents for anything was when he borrowed money for his first car just before he got married. They told him he would have to pay them back a little money each month, and he did so without any further prompting.

For the first twenty-one years of his life, J.C. never hurt anyone. He attended church regularly as a youngster, and was even an altar boy until he entered the eighth grade. He was thought of as a quiet, well-mannered, and gentle young man. His basketball coach remembers that J.C. was afraid to play hard during practice for fear of hurting one of his teammates, since he was so much bigger than they were. His high school principal recalls that he was "helpful to the smaller students in the school, and would always lend a helping hand when and where needed." Many of the letters later written on J.C.'s behalf described him as a "good boy" who "didn't have a mean bone in his body." In 1985, days before his scheduled execution, J.C. was asked by a reporter how he wanted to be remembered:

> **I'm just sort of easygoing and if you need help, I'll give you the shirt off my back. I don't know if I will be remembered by too many people in this state other than for what they believe I am**

now. But for my friends and family, I just want to be remembered for being a family member. And I hope that anybody who can remember my past can forget what happened seven years ago.

. . . .

J.C. had always wanted to join the Army. He finally enlisted after his first year of marriage, but was turned down when a physical examination revealed a cyst at the base of his spine. Not to be deterred, he had an operation to remove the cyst and reapplied. After basic training at Fort Knox, Kentucky, J.C. was stationed at Fort Jackson in Columbia, South Carolina. He soon developed an interest in the Military Police (MP), and sought admission to the Military Police school at Fort Gordon, in Savannah, Georgia. He graduated on May 14, 1975.

At first, J.C. loved the Army. The official photo of J.C. in his MP uniform shows a man who was proud to serve his country. And the Army was pleased with him as well. On December 15, 1976, he received a letter of commendation for his work at Fort Jackson.

J.C.'s disillusionment with the Army began with his discovery that he was not being paid the amount to which he was entitled. It took a long time to straighten out his salary, and J.C. grew increasingly frustrated with the Army's bureaucracy. Even after his pay was corrected, he and Karyn had trouble meeting their financial obligations. In addition, J.C. never got the promotion that he was due as a result of his letter of commendation. What cemented his dismay with the Army, however, and hastened his attempts to secure his release, was Karyn's miscarriage. For reasons that are still unclear, Karyn and J.C. were denied treatment at the base hospital when J.C. rushed Karyn there for the pains she was experiencing early in her pregnancy. As J.C. later described it, "The Army wouldn't treat her. They said she was pregnant when I took her to the emergency room. They said we had to go to the Ob/Gyn because she was pregnant, and they couldn't do nothing for her." By the time they arrived at the nearby hospital to which they were referred, Karyn had lost the baby.

Both J.C. and Karyn were grief-stricken by their loss. They were also faced with mounting bills. Shortly after the miscarriage, J.C. was involved in an unfortunate incident that ended up costing him his job as an M.P.

He was riding in a friend's car, and they were stopped upon arriving at Fort Jackson, under suspicion of transporting drugs. J.C. protested his innocence, but was advised to sign an Article 15, the Army's version of a plea, rather than risk a court-martial. The presiding colonel ended up dropping the case, saying there was no evidence to justify stopping J.C. and his friend in the first place. But J.C.'s company commander demoted him because he had signed the Article 15. J.C. was no longer allowed to carry a gun or be a posted guard. In order to make ends meet, Karyn took a waitressing job at a nearby Shoney's restaurant. She soon began an affair with the assistant manager there, which J.C. inadvertently learned about from his stepfather.

"Money's so tight that Karyn has to work double shifts," he told Robert Sr. on the phone one day. "Lately she goes in at 5:00 A.M. and doesn't get home until the following night."

"Sounds like she's fooling around on you, son," Robert Sr. told him, but J.C. didn't want to hear it.

"Oh no, she would never do that," he insisted.

A few days later, he called back, totally crestfallen. He had seen the assistant manager driving his and Karyn's car, and that was all the confirmation he needed. He and Karyn separated.

Robert and Mary knew their son was depressed. Karyn had been his whole life, and the separation devastated him. Mary worried about him, but Robert always reassured her. "There's no better place he can be, honey," he'd say. "The Army takes care of its soldiers. They'll look after him."

Karyn moved back home to Kentucky. J.C. did just about everything he could to try to get her to come back. He called her incessantly, often in the middle of the night. He also reached out to her sister and mother, both of whom liked J.C., asking them to try to convince Karyn to return to him.

After Karyn left him, a married couple with whom J.C. was friendly moved in to help him with the rent. J.C., who had always let Karyn handle the bills, was happy to comply with the arrangement they proposed of giving them his share of the rent and letting them take care of everything. The landlord's eviction notice, giving J.C. ten days to vacate the premises for nonpayment of rent, arrived the same day his so-called friends disappeared. J.C. returned home a few days later to find all of his clothes and furniture gone. Not knowing where else to turn, he moved back to Fort Jackson and to the Army life he now hated.

. . . .

The first indication Robert and Mary Crum had that the Army was not, in fact, looking out for their son was a call they received from J.C.'s new housemate in August 1977. For a second time, J.C. had taken an overdose of sleeping pills. The military hospital pumped his stomach but did not admit him for observation.

Mary, who was terrified of flying, got on the next plane to go get J.C. She instinctively knew he would be okay if she could just get him home, but the most the Army would agree to was a three-day pass.

At first, all J.C. wanted to do was sleep. "They've got me so doped up," he kept saying. But "the kids" soon had J.C. back to his old self, wrestling in the basement and cracking jokes. When Robert Sr. drove J.C. to the airport at the end of the three days, he was relieved to note that J.C. seemed to be in good spirits.

"I know you're having a hard time with Karyn leaving you, but there are other fish in the sea," Robert Sr. assured him. "You're a good-looking guy. You'll get over this."

J.C. nodded in agreement, not wanting to dispel his stepfather's misguided belief that he shared his optimism. Earlier, he had tried to convince Robert Jr. to go back with him to Fort Jackson and stay a while, but he had declined. Much later, reflecting on J.C.'s request, Robert Jr. regretted his decision to stay behind.

The next time the family saw J.C. was in early October 1977. Contact with him had been sporadic since his three-day visit in August, and Mary was distressed that J.C. had not even bothered to call her on her birthday. She had fumed about it all day, but was delighted to find J.C. at home waiting for her when she returned from work. He was in high spirits because Karyn, with whom he had been trying to reconcile, had agreed to go back to Fort Jackson with him. On the day before he was due to leave, Karyn called and said she had changed her mind. That ended the visit. J.C. left in a hurry, barely managing to say good-bye. The Crums later learned that J.C. had been AWOL (absent without leave).

Shortly after this visit, the Crums moved from Jefferstown, Kentucky, to Pee Wee Valley, in the same state. Robert Sr. wrote J.C. informing him of the move and assuring him that he would always have a home with them.

. . . .

Throughout the year following his separation, J.C. received counseling at the Fort Jackson Mental Health Center. Depression was not J.C.'s only problem. He told his parents that he needed to see a doctor about his ears. When they asked him what exactly was wrong with his ears, he responded, "What people are saying is not what I am hearing." He also turned to drugs and alcohol, experimenting with marijuana, cocaine, PCP, LSD, crystal methadone, mushrooms, speed, downers—anything he could.

Every morning, J.C. would wake up and smoke several joints on the way to work. When he came home for lunch, he would take Percodan and Valium, which helped him get through the rest of the workday. On his way home, he would pick up a case of beer, which he and his roommate would consume along with whatever drugs happened to be available. As he later described it, "The only way I could live with myself was not to live with myself."

His circle of friends spent their time together getting high. J.C., twenty-two at this point, shared a house with Robert Neil Williams, one year his junior. The two were often visited by James Terry Roach, a seventeen-year-old, and Ronald Eugene Mahaffey, a sixteen-year-old. Even though J.C. was the oldest, he was not the leader; that role was filled by Roach. The four could often be found at J.C.'s and Robert's home, sharing the drugs that they had purchased together.

J.C.'s misery was given a brief respite when he began a relationship with a woman with whom he worked. The relationship progressed quickly, allowing J.C. to begin to envision a life without Karyn. His new girlfriend left the Army so that she could move in with J.C., and they began to look at rings together. But before J.C. could present her with the ring, she left. Perhaps it was because of his drug use; although it was tempered when he was with her, it never ceased. Perhaps it was because he still heard voices telling him what to do, particularly when he was tripping on PCP. Perhaps it was because he was still obsessed with Karyn. For whatever reason, the relationship ended abruptly on October 16, 1977.

J.C.'s only coping mechanism at this point was losing himself in drugs and alcohol, which he did all that night and the following day. As he did so, the voices intensified. They told him to get back at Karyn and all women who could hurt him. They told him to get revenge. Williams, Roach, and Mahaffey were also there, sharing his drugs and his rage. By nightfall on October 17, 1977, their drug-induced ranting evolved into a plan to go out and find a woman to rape.

. . . .

Betty Swank's life had not been an easy one. Shuffled from one foster family to another, she longed for stability and love. She found what she was after in Albert Swank, whom she married at age sixteen. By the time she was twenty-one, she was the proud mother of a fifteen-month-old son. She finally had the family she had craved growing up. But the marriage was not without its problems. Betty and Albert were struggling on Albert's meager military salary, and to help make ends meet, Betty reluctantly took the night shift at a manufacturing plant. Jittery by nature, she hated driving at night. She usually picked up a friend who shared her midnight shift so that she wouldn't have to drive alone.

On October 17, 1977, Betty left her home as usual to pick up her friend. She never made it. Thinking that her tire had suddenly blown out, Betty pulled into the parking lot of Roach's Market. The tire had actually been shot out by the four men who offered to give her a ride to her friend's house. Once inside the car, she saw the gun hidden under the back seat, but it was too late. She was kidnapped, raped, and shot. She was found murdered in the same mobile home park where her own trailer was located, shot twice with a .22 caliber pistol. She had made the mistake of recognizing one of her captors. "Aren't you stationed at Fort Jackson with my husband?" she asked J.C. Shaw.

After they had all raped Betty, they offered her a ride home. She accepted, thinking that the worst had already happened to her. She asked if she could sit up front with J.C., telling him he was the only one she felt she could trust. J.C. dropped her off where she had requested, thinking as he did so that she looked a lot like Karyn. He drove about a hundred yards before the voices started in, prodding him to kill her. J.C. swerved the car around and returned to Betty. He called her over to the car, pulling out his gun as she approached. His three friends in the back yelled out in surprise as he shot her, but at least the voices were quiet.

. . . .

Earline Raffield, the receptionist at the Fort Jackson Mental Health Clinic, saw many troubled young men. But on Friday, October 28, 1977, there was something particularly urgent about the young soldier who came in pleading to be committed. He was dressed in civilian clothes and identified himself as J.C. Shaw.

"I've got to see a psychiatrist," he said repeatedly. "He's got to put me on the ward."

Raffield referred him to one of the psychiatrists on duty, who saw the distraught man for approximately fifteen minutes before sending him on his way.

That afternoon, the man returned, even more visibly upset than before.

"I've *got* to see somebody," he pleaded with her. "I'm afraid of what might happen. I'm afraid of what I might do."

Raffield was the only staff member on duty. The rest of the Mental Health Clinic staff was in the backyard, enjoying a beer and hotdog party. Impressed with J.C.'s desperation and urgency, Earline went outside to the party and interrupted the festivities. She explained to Lieutenant Spradlin, a social worker, that this was Mr. Shaw's second visit to the clinic that day and his second request for help.

J.C. was again seen for fifteen minutes before being dismissed. As he left through the reception area, Raffield found herself wishing they could have done more for him.

. . . .

Carlotta Hartness and Tommy Taylor were boyfriend and girlfriend, and the two teenagers seemed to have a lot in common. They attended a highly regarded private school about five miles north of where Betty Swank was murdered. Both came from wealthy families prominent in Richland County, South Carolina. And both fourteen-year-old Carlotta and seventeen-year-old Tommy were unusually dependable and responsible.

On Saturday, October 29, 1977, the teens took off in Tommy's white Oldsmobile to do some research for a school paper Tommy was writing about his county's beautiful historic district. When neither Carlotta nor Tommy had telephoned by that evening to explain why they were late, their parents knew something was wrong. At 3:55 A.M. the next morning, their fears were confirmed. Tommy was found slumped over on the front seat of his car, shot twice in the head. At 2:30 P.M. that afternoon, Carlotta's mutilated corpse was discovered in a wooded area northwest of Columbia.

She had been shot five times in the back of the head and raped. The autopsy revealed that a number of injuries were also inflicted on her body post-mortem.

> *The voices were at it again. They told J.C. to go back to the dead girl's body and tear it up. Doing so would relieve this terrible pressure. They promised him he would feel the same relief he felt after shooting Betty Swank; that same sense of fulfilling an obligation. When he arrived at the spot in the woods where they'd left her to die, he was actually surprised to see her. She still looked alive, and J.C. was half expecting her to sit up and ask him why they had done those terrible things to her. He closed her eyes, knowing he couldn't do what he was supposed to do to her with her staring at him, even in death. The voices then guided him to a broken bottle nearby, which he used to do the things to her that they told him to do.*

. . . .

Robert Jr. was the one who answered the phone. He could tell right away there was something wrong with J.C. He called to his father to take the upstairs line. Robert Sr., upon hearing it was J.C., was relieved that he had called. He was sure it was in response to the letter he had sent J.C. about the move. When he picked up, however, J.C. had something entirely different to discuss. Robert Jr. listened on the downstairs line while J.C. told his stepfather that he was in jail for murdering three people.

At first, Robert Sr. was convinced that this was yet another one of J.C.'s practical jokes. "Come on, J.C." he kept saying. "Stop fooling around." But Robert Jr. knew all along that it was no joke. He could just tell.

Robert Sr. kept telling J.C. not to hang up. "Your mother's due home from work any minute now, and I want her to hear this from you, not me."

When Mary walked up the front steps, Robert Jr. ran out to meet her at the front door. "J.C.'s on the phone," he said breathlessly. "He's in jail."

Once his parents hung up the phone, Robert Jr. could hear them still trying to convince themselves that it was all a joke and that J.C. would be calling back any minute. They even went so far as to call the South Carolina jail from which J.C. had ostensibly called to make sure he was actually being held there. He could tell when they finally accepted the terrible news because they were both suddenly very quiet.

Robert Jr. went into his room and shut the door. He sat on the edge of the bed in the room he had shared with his big brother. He put his face in his hands and cried.

· · · · · · · ·

Soon the Crums' neighbors and relatives arrived at the house. They tried to console the devastated family, but they were all too shocked themselves to offer much comfort. Uncle Charlie focused on the practical issue of J.C.'s legal representation.

"You don't want him to have one of those court-appointed attorneys," he insisted. "They're no good. You need to hire a first-rate lawyer."

Uncle Charlie didn't know anyone in South Carolina, but he knew a local attorney who could probably recommend someone. Through him, Robert and Mary got the name of an experienced criminal lawyer in South Carolina, who agreed to look into the case for five hundred dollars. It was a lot of money, but it would be worth it if it helped them get their son back. The attorney met with Robert Sr. a few days later and told them he was willing to take the case. He informed him that he couldn't get J.C. off, but he could guarantee that J.C. wouldn't get the death penalty.

"How much?" Robert Sr. asked.

"Twenty thousand dollars, up front."

Robert Sr. was stunned. He had no hope of getting that kind of money together. The Crums had had a hard enough time coming up with the initial five hundred dollars. They reluctantly said farewell to the recommended attorney—and their five hundred dollars—and tried instead to reassure themselves about J.C.'s court-appointed counsel. He was, after all, a prominent local attorney. The case had received so much publicity that the judge had appointed Kermit S. King, a successful and highly regarded member of the South Carolina bar, to represent J.C. Unbeknownst to the Crums, however, King's reputation was built on his record as a divorce attorney. This was not only his first capital case, but his first criminal case of any kind.

· · · · · · · ·

Mary didn't know whether or not the room was bugged. It would explain why J.C. was acting so strangely. She was prepared for him to break down and cry or pound his fist in anger, but she didn't know what to do with this stiff and wooden stranger. When she hugged him, it was like hugging a fencepost. He had barely spoken to them since they had arrived at the jail. She told him to write down whether he'd really done those awful things. She was sure he was simply scared that they would use whatever he said against him. That's why he was being so quiet. But J.C. never even picked up the pen and paper she proffered.

Robert and Mary tried to talk to King, but he made it clear he would not discuss the case with them. "You're not the client," he informed them. "J.C. is." They soon learned that this meant they could not have any input on his decisions or case strategy. They wanted to talk to King about his approach to the case. They didn't understand why he was encouraging J.C. to plead guilty. They knew their understanding of the law was murky at best, but they could not comprehend how J.C. would benefit from pleading guilty to the exact crimes with which he was charged. They wanted to ask him why he wasn't going to let J.C. go before a jury. Surely that would be better than letting a single man decide his fate, a man who, it was later revealed, had aspirations for higher office and was handling a highly publicized case. But the Crums' opinions were neither sought nor welcomed. King's insistence on a plea so early on in the case, with minimal investigation and a client whom King himself described as "a functional mute," was apparently based on King's belief that the only way J.C. could get a life sentence rather than the death penalty would be for the judge to accept his plea.

"I gave Judge Harwell a leather jacket last year for Christmas," King told J.C. "So he owes me one."

The whole family came down for the plea. Gregory did not want to go. He had been acting out at school since the night J.C. called from jail. Once they arrived in South Carolina, Dennis wanted to go home. Only Robert Jr. wanted to be there. He didn't understand what had happened to J.C., why his big brother was acting like he had a shell around him. But he still wanted to be with him.

When J.C. pled guilty to the Hartness and Taylor murders, he did so with the stipulation that he did not pull the trigger. Mary was able to draw some consolation from the fact that Judge Harwell accepted J.C.'s plea. That must mean he believed her son. J.C. may have been there, but he didn't do the actual killings. King later confirmed to the Crums that J.C. had steadfastly maintained that he had not shot either of the teens, but that he had admitted to killing Betty Swank. The murder pleas were entered on the theory that J.C. was guilty of felony murder under the doctrine that the "hand of one is the hand of all."

J.C. never testified or made a statement at his brief sentencing hearing. He did not contest codefendant Ronald Eugene Mahaffey's testimony that it was James Terry Roach who shot both victims, but that J.C. had taken a final shot at Carlotta Hartness after Roach had shot her several times.

At one point, Judge Harwell asked J.C. if he had anything to say. "Yes," J.C. responded. He wanted to express to the judge how bad he felt about what had happened. He wanted to tell him that the relief he'd felt after the crimes was now replaced with shame and regret. He wanted to say he was sorry. But before he could articulate any of those things, his lawyer jumped in.

"He has nothing to say, your Honor," he pronounced. "He misunderstood the question."

It all happened so fast. Only six weeks elapsed from the time the crimes were committed to the time J.C. was sentenced to death. At his sentencing, J.C. sat as if in a trance. His brothers all watched him and marveled at how perfectly still he sat. He stared straight ahead and never changed his position throughout the entire proceeding. The newspapers all described him as "wooden" and "without any signs of remorse." His court-appointed attorneys (who included, in addition to Kermit King, Dallas D. Ball and W. Thomas Vernon) were quoted as saying that J.C. was "an exceedingly difficult man to talk with and to communicate with."

Much later, when the psychiatrists who had observed and evaluated J.C. between his plea and his sentencing reported their findings, it was clear J.C. was neither mute nor intentionally uncommunicative. He was suffering from a severe case of clinical depression.

. . . .

J.C. was committed to a mental health hospital on November 10, 1977, pursuant to a court order. Dr. Harold Morgan, a psychiatric consultant to the South Carolina state hospital, observed J.C. for three weeks between his arrest and his plea. The other psychiatrists who examined him after his arrest concurred with Dr. Morgan's assessment. They diagnosed J.C. as suffering from latent schizophrenia, alcoholism, drug abuse, and emotional disturbance. These mental disorders caused J.C. to suffer hallucinations, delusional thinking, severe depression, and extreme difficulty in communicating. Dr. Morgan later testified at J.C.'s postconviction relief proceeding that J.C. lacked the ability to make his own independent and reasoned choices in deciding to plead guilty. He told the judge:

> From the beginning, I have felt that Mr. Shaw is basically schizophrenic. The primary sign of this is his detachment, that is, the classical "split" between thinking and feeling. I have never seen J.C. Shaw express any kind of emotion. It must be noted that these are subtle signs. He does not have the more florid signs such as hallucinations and delusions which would be necessary to confirm the diagnosis for legal purposes. Alcohol and drugs, which have a disinhibiting effect, increase the likelihood that his suppressed feelings will be unleashed. I think this is what happened in 1977.

J.C. attempted suicide for a third time while at the mental hospital. On December 12, 1977, less than two weeks after his return to jail from the hospital and on the advice of his court-appointed attorneys, J.C. Shaw entered pleas of guilty to all the charges he was facing. The charges, which pertained only to the Hartness and Taylor murders, included two counts of murder, two counts of conspiracy, rape, kidnapping, and armed robbery. The state chose to try J.C. first for the teens' murders, which generated far more publicity and public outcry than did Betty Swank's murder. He later pleaded guilty to the charges associated with Betty Swank's death, for which he was sentenced to life in prison.

. . . .

J.C. Shaw was the first person in South Carolina to face the death penalty after capital punishment was temporarily outlawed in the early 1970s. Prior to his sentencing, the court conducted a presentencing hearing as required by a recently enacted South Carolina death penalty statute. The statute requires that prior to imposing the death penalty, the judge (regardless of whether the sentencing authority is the court or the jury) must find as an affirmative fact that the death penalty is warranted under the evidence and is not imposed as the result of prejudice, passion, or any other arbitrary factor.

Judge David Harwell, sitting without a jury, heard evidence regarding extenuation, mitigation, and aggravation. He found that three of the statutory aggravating circumstances were present: Murder was committed while in the commission of rape; murder was committed while in the commission of kidnapping, and murder was committed while in the commission of armed robbery. In mitigation, the judge found that J.C. had no significant history of prior criminal activity involving the use of violence against another person, that the murder was committed while J.C. was under the influence of extreme mental or emotional disturbance, and that J.C.'s capacity to conform his conduct to the requirements of the law was substantially impaired. The judge also found that J.C.'s age and mentality at the time of the crime were mitigating factors.

The state was permitted, over the objections of J.C.'s counsel, to introduce seven photographs into evidence. These photos depicted the scene of the crime and J.C.'s postmortem abuse of Carlotta Hartness's body. There were three photos of her body at the scene of the murder, one close-up of the disfigurement to her left breast, another of the disfigurement to her pubic area, a photograph of a piece of glass removed from her pubic area, and one of a tampon found at the scene of the murder. Judge Harwell decreed that these photos were admissible not only as a circumstance of the crime, but also as evidence of J.C.'s character.

On December 16, 1977, Judge Harwell imposed a sentence of death upon Joseph Carl Shaw. James Terry Roach was sentenced later, also to death. In exchange for his testimony against Shaw and Roach, Donald Eugene Mahaffey received a life sentence. Robert Neil Williams, whose involvement was limited to Betty Swank's murder, was not a defendant in the Hartness and Taylor cases. In a separate trial, he was later given a life sentence for his role in Betty Swank's murder.

. . . .

When he returned to Kentucky after the sentencing, Robert Jr. resolved not to discuss his brother with anyone. He kept telling himself that he wasn't ashamed, but it wasn't something he was proud of either. At first, it wasn't hard keeping quiet about J.C. No one seemed to connect him with the notorious South Carolina murderer because he and J.C. did not have the same last name. Adding to his anonymity was the fact that the Crums had recently moved from J.C.'s childhood home of Jefferstown, Kentucky, to Pee Wee Valley.

But one story in the local paper identified J.C. as the son of Robert and Mary Crum, which devastated Mary. Even more troubling was the article about J.C. and his "killing spree" in the magazine *True Detective*, which was published in October 1978. Entitled, "Murder Climaxed the Gang's Fun and Games," the article seemed to crystallize for Mary all the shame and despair she felt about what had happened to her oldest son. She purchased every copy of the magazine she could find in the vain hope of trying to keep her neighbors from reading the article.

Robert Jr. ended his silence about his big brother during his ninth-grade civics class. The topic of the day was the death penalty. Robert Jr. and his classmates were instructed to stand on opposite sides of the room, reflecting their personal views on the issue. The blackboard wall represented those who were opposed to the death penalty, and the opposite wall represented those who were in favor of it. Robert Jr. was the only student in his entire class who stood in front of the blackboard. Looking across at his classmates, who stared at him in a mixture of consternation and defiance, Robert Jr. began to cry. He cried so hard and for so long that Mr. Craig, his teacher, had to escort him from the classroom. Despite Mr. Craig's gentle prodding, Robert Jr. would not divulge why he was crying. Later, one of his classmates approached him in the hallway.

"Is your brother that big murderer in South Carolina?" he asked.

"Yup," Robert Jr. said, after a pause. He looked the kid right in the eyes. "He is."

Nothing else was ever said to Robert Jr. about J.C.

A few years later, Dennis experienced the identical ostracizing phenomenon when his ninth-grade civics class tackled the death penalty. He didn't have the benefit of Robert Jr.'s wisdom or advice, however, because the two brothers had never discussed J.C. or his impact on their lives. Later, when J.C. was on Death Row, Dennis would find himself wincing when his friends, oblivious to his vulnerability, would make hostile comments about local criminals, such as "They ought to hang the bastard," or "He deserves to have his dick sliced off."

One day, Dennis confronted them in the most nonconfrontational way he could. "Look," he said, "I know I'm giving you a biased view, but you need to know that normal people are on the other side. The difference between me and J.C. is very small. I don't know what makes you go over the edge, but something does. It could happen to anyone. So when you talk about revenge, think to yourself, 'What if it were one of my loved ones?' Because I love J.C. more than anything."

. . . .

In 1979, the Kentucky Coalition Against the Death Penalty flew Robert and Mary Crum to South Carolina in an effort to convince J.C. not to drop his appeals. It seemed that J.C. had simply had enough. He no longer had any hope that his appeals would be successful and that his sentence would be commuted. Even the best possible outcome—spending the rest of his life in prison—was difficult to accept. Robert Sr. told him that dropping his appeals was tantamount to committing suicide, and he wondered whether that was, in fact, J.C.'s intent.

J.C. also toyed with other options during this time, as evidenced by his letters home to his brother, mother, and his cousin Debbie.

Feb. 18

Dear Robert,

What it is! Hey, your car looks great, my first car was 5 years old and my second was 7 so its almost turned around for you, your first one was almost 7 and this one is 5. The color looks OK to me. Well I guess you'll have the house to yourself this weekend or right after, whats Robyn say about that. Ha. Caught you didn't I! Ha. Ha.

I guess it does cost a arm and a leg to go to college, so the money you make working full time will help out. Nothing much going on here, same old thing every day, that's why there's nothing ever to write about. I'm doing OK, but I guess you've talked to Debbie about what I've been telling her, I don't know how you feel about it but it's something that I just have to try. I know you might not understand it but I'm tired of staying in this place and I'm not going to. I don't know how everybody knows something's up but don't say anything to Mom and Dad cause it will just worry them. I don't want to let anybody down but I just can't spend the rest of my life in here.

Take Care,
Love, Your Brother,
J.C.

March 5

Dear Debbie,

How you doing? I'm OK. How's your new job working out? Ok, I'll run it down to you so you'll know what's going on. When I asked you to *see if you could find those 3 people for me I was going to try and get them to come down here and get me out, but since you can't get a hold of them thats out now. I had things set up so that it wouldn't be any trouble at all for them or me. So now that I can't seem to get any help on the outside I'm trying to get up $500 or at least half that much, with that money I'll be able to sorta buy my way out, I know it sounds crazy but it can be done without anybody getting hurt. My appeal was supposed to be heard in Feb. but it wasn't so it will most likely be this month and if I get turned down my lawyers want to go on to another court but I'm not going to, Mom and everybody thinks that I'm going to do what my lawyers say but I'm not and if I told them what I'm trying to do I don't think they would go along with it cause they will think I'll get killed or some thing. So in other words if I don't get the money from somewhere I'm going to drop my appeal and let the state go ahead and do its thing.*

I wrote and told Robert that I wasn't going to stay in here the rest of my life but I didn't tell it to him just like I did you now.

It was good to see everybody when they came down but mom kept saying that things would get better in the other court, so I had to lie and say yeah, ok, I know, when all the time I knew I wasn't going to go there. I know it's a strange thing to here but if I told anybody else but Robert I don't know what they would do. Being free and on the run would be a lot better than spending the rest of my life in here. So that's how it is. I don't want you to get in any trouble over this, you here me!

> *Take care,*
> *Love, J.C.*

March 25

Dear Mom,

Got your letter today. I won't say anything to Debbie about it. Your a good mother so don't go thinking that your not, it's not your fault or anybody else's. I don't remember everything I said in Debbie's letter but I think I have a chance to get out, I wrote Ann about it Friday and if I get the chance I'm going to take it. I know how you feel about that but I don't have any other choice. I don't want to hurt any of you but I'm not going to spend the rest of my life in here. I don't know if things would change even if I get out but just thinking and sitting in here about what I did just wears me out and I can't take it anymore. You or nobody else really knows me, it's nobody's fault, I act different around different people, maybe I just don't like people.

I don't want it to sound like I'm saying "either help me get out or I'm going to drop my appeal" but that's about it. If you think its against your belief to help me get out then don't do it, I won't be mad or feel you don't love me, I don't want it to sound like blackmail.

I don't know when I'll here about the decision on my appeal but I can't see having John Delgado spend any more money on another appeal when I don't want it.

It's not that I don't love you all, but I'm not going to live the rest of my life in here. They won't send me back to Kentucky besides it would still be 20 years till parole.

I'm sorry I had to say all of this but it's the way it is.

Love,

J.C.

The entire family tried to prevail upon J.C. not to abandon his appeals. Dennis, who was sixteen at the time, wrote, "I wish and pray you don't do this. You probably think I and everyone else will get over it. Your wrong, J.C."

Contributing to J.C.'s distress was the regret and shame he felt about his crimes. Many of the letters written on J.C.'s behalf in an attempt to save his life referred to his deep remorse. Pat Murray, a prison teacher, wrote: "Atoning for those crimes preoccupied him in the first several months of his incarceration. It was a long time before he could accept the fact that his atonement need not take the form of his own death."

Mary McFadden, a prison volunteer who spent many hours talking with J.C., recalled his telling her around the time he considered dropping his appeals that he had relived the murders a certain number of times. When she later checked his file, she realized the number of times he cited was the exact number of days since the murders had occurred.

It was not his relatives, however, who were able to convince J.C. to continue to pursue his case. The credit goes to Father Duffy, the prison chaplain, and Frankie-San, the prison librarian. Both gained J.C.'s trust and respect and were ultimately able to change his mind. They helped J.C. realize that he could still contribute to society from within prison, and that his life was still worth something.

. . . .

Once again breaking ground, J.C. Shaw's case was the first capital case reviewed by the South Carolina Supreme Court under the state's new death penalty statute. By law, the court undertook a mandatory review of J.C.'s death sentence in consolidation with his direct appeal of that sentence. Rejecting all of his and codefendant Roach's arguments for setting the sentence aside, the four sitting members of the court affirmed the sentences of death.

Shaw and Roach contended that the solicitor's decision to seek the death penalty against them was arbitrary and capricious in view of his decision not to seek the death penalty against Mahaffey. The court disagreed, finding that there was a basis for distinguishing Mahaffey from Shaw and Roach that rendered him less deserving of the punishment his codefendants received. Unlike Shaw and Roach, Mahaffey was not a triggerman in the murders. More important, however, the state needed Mahaffey's testimony in order to bolster its case against Shaw and Roach.

J.C.'s appeal also found fault with the statutory circumstances of mitigation and arbitration cited by Judge Harwell, arguing that they should have been assigned numerical values and that they were arbitrary classifications. The court, maintaining that the classifications were not arbitrary on their face, concluded that the state's death penalty statute was constitutional and a sentence of death could be lawfully imposed. The court also summarily rejected the arguments that the method of execution by electrocution constituted cruel and unusual punishment and that the state's introduction of evidence in aggravation of punishment, particularly the photos, was inflammatory and prejudicial.

As part of its mandatory sentence review, the court determined that the sentences of death conformed to the statutory requirements. After reviewing the entire record and transcript, the report of the trial judge, and the arguments of trial counsel, the court concluded that (1) the sentences of death were not imposed under the influence of passion, prejudice, or any other arbitrary factor; (2) the evidence supported the sentencing authority's findings of statutory aggravating circumstances; (3) the sentence of death was not excessive or disproportionate to the penalty imposed in similar cases, considering both the crime and the defendant.

On November 13, 1979, the U.S. Supreme Court denied the writ of certiorari in the case of *State v. Shaw*. The highest court in the nation was essentially declining to pass judgment on J.C.'s death sentence. The South Carolina Supreme Court wasted little time in directing that the sentence of death be imposed. On November 21, 1979, the execution of J.C. Shaw was scheduled for December 14, 1979.

. . . .

Robert and Mary Crum flew down to Columbia, South Carolina, for what they were told would be a routine appeal of their son's case. Even though they wanted to trust King and believe that there was nothing to worry about, they could tell that things were not going according to plan. There was a sense of urgency surrounding everyone involved with J.C.'s case. It was clear they were scrambling to get something done. Robert and Mary were shuffled around from one interview to another, but they were never given a straight answer as to what was going on.

The Crums were right to worry. J.C.'s court-appointed counsel commenced federal and state postconviction proceedings on December 11, 1979. The following day, they filed a petition seeking a writ of habeas corpus in the U.S. district court and a Motion for a Stay of Execution. That same day, the district court held a hearing and denied the stay.

Fortunately for J.C., another important development in his case took place that day. Richard Burr, a staff attorney with the Southern Prisoners' Defense Commission, flew from Nashville to Columbia to meet with J.C. He had received an urgent call from Mary McFadden, a prison volunteer and ardent opponent of the death penalty, alerting him to J.C.'s dire situation and asking Burr to save J.C. Burr convinced J.C. to allow him and two local attorneys, Kenneth Suggs and John Delgado, to take over the case. They did so on a purely pro bono basis, since the petition Kermit King had filed that day represented the final legal appeal that qualified for state funds. At 9:30 P.M. on December 12, 1979, J.C.'s new counsel filed a supplemental petition for a writ of habeas corpus and a Motion for Stay of Execution stating new grounds for relief. In particular, they asserted that J.C. had received ineffective assistance of counsel from his trial and appellate counsel in violation of the Sixth and Fourteenth Amendments to the United States Constitution.

J.C.'s attorneys were not the only ones who were frantically busy. The prison officials were also busy reviewing the recently devised procedures for executions, since J.C.'s was the first one scheduled in South Carolina in more than twenty years. J.C. was moved to the Death House, which was designed to house prisoners at South Carolina's Central Correctional Institution (CCI) until their executions.

Robert couldn't put his finger on what was different about J.C., but he definitely sensed a change in his stepson. It was a subtle change; not even Mary could detect what Robert perceived, but it bothered Robert that he couldn't identify what it was. One night, the stress of the press interviews, being shuffled around, and the mounting awkwardness between him and J.C. got to Robert. He chose not to accompany Mary to the prison; he just couldn't handle it. Mary returned that night to report that J.C. was very upset by Robert's absence.

Eighteen hours before the scheduled time for the execution, the Honorable Judge Dickson Phillips, a judge on the U.S. Court of Appeals for the Fourth Circuit, granted a stay, pending the outcome of state and federal collateral proceedings. Robert, noting J.C.'s visible relief, finally put his finger on what had been different about J.C.: fear. J.C. Shaw was scared to death of death—a death that, until then, had seemed increasingly imminent and inevitable.

When Robert and Mary returned home to Kentucky, Robert still felt distressed and disoriented. Mary found him sitting on the bed, his head in his hands. Despite having already missed work because of the trip to South Carolina, Robert called his boss and told him he was too sick to come in that day. He did not feel any better as the day progressed. That night he complained of chest pains. Mary called 911, and an ambulance soon arrived to rush Robert to the hospital. The doctors who examined him in the emergency room told him he was on the verge of having a heart attack. He was given Valium and felt significantly better the following day. His doctor told him to avoid stress; his nerves couldn't take it.

· · · · · · · ·

On January 28, 1980, a hearing was held in the Court of Common Pleas of Richland County, South Carolina, before Judge Rodney Peoples in response to J.C.'s application for postconviction relief. Even though Judge Phillips had granted the stay in federal court, J.C. was required by law to first present his claims to the state court before the federal court could review them. Prior to the hearing, Gerry Spence, a nationally renowned defense attorney, was admitted, pro hac vice (allowing him to practice in the state even though he was not a member of the South Carolina bar), to represent J.C. Spence flew in from Wyoming to serve as lead counsel at the evidentiary hearing.

It took eight days for Spence to present the facts and testimony in support of J.C.'s claim that his court-appointed trial and appellate counsel did not provide the type of representation reasonably expected of a criminal trial attorney. In particular, Spence asserted that Kermit King knew that Judge Harwell, the judge before whom J.C. had pled guilty, was in favor of the death penalty. He presented evidence that Judge Harwell had apprised counsel of his pro–death penalty record as a legislator during a pretrial conference, but Kermit King neglected to inform J.C. of the judge's predisposition when advising him to plead guilty. Adding to Judge Harwell's own support of the death penalty was the political pressure he felt to sentence J.C. to death. Spence presented evidence that South Carolina Supreme Court Justice "Bubba" Ness had told Judge Harwell that if he did not give J.C. death, he would be holding court in Walhalla for the rest of his life.

Spence also elicited a great deal of testimony about J.C. as a person, in particular his childhood, marriage, and drug use, since very little was revealed about him prior to his plea and sentencing. Far from the mute and inarticulate defendant he had appeared to be at previous court appearances, J.C. was able to express the deep remorse he felt for the crimes he had committed.

"If I had knew what I was doing at the time, it never would have happened, and I feel real bad for their families, and I wish there was some way that I could make it all work out right," J.C. said at the evidentiary proceeding.

"If you could give your life to make it work out right," Spence asked him. "Would you do that?"

"I would," J.C. replied emphatically.

Another emotional moment came when J.C. was asked about his relationship with his brothers. In conveying how much he loved them, J.C. began to sob, prompting the judge to call a recess. Mary remembers that moment as the first time she saw J.C. cry following the murders.

On February 7, 1980, at the conclusion of the eight days of testimony and arguments, Judge Peoples entered an order from the bench denying relief. In his denial, he seemed to take offense at the insinuation that J.C.'s trial counsel had been at all deficient, stating that "Kermit King is one of the top five lawyers in South Carolina" and that he was "the finest representation that money could buy." He therefore decreed that, "Every ground, issue, and allegation presented by Petitioner in this postconviction relief proceeding is hereby dismissed and denied as being without merit."

Without wasting any time bemoaning Judge Peoples's total dismissal of all the allegations raised, J.C., through Dick Burr (the Southern Prisoners' Defense Commission attorney), Kenneth Suggs, and John Delgado, immediately appealed to the South Carolina Supreme Court. On April 1, 1981, that court also denied his appeal. Later that month, on April 21, J.C.'s motion for a rehearing was denied. On April 24, the South Carolina Supreme Court set a new execution date of May 22, 1981. A flurry of motions followed, including the state's application to the U.S. district court for a dissolution of the stay entered by Judge Phillips in 1979 and a request by J.C. for an additional stay in the district court. On May 15, the district court granted a writ of mandamus and issued an opinion reaffirming its stay of execution and amending it to apply to the execution set for May 22, 1981.

Every defendant who is sentenced to death has several opportunities to have his case reviewed. He can appeal directly after his trial, as J.C. did unsuccessfully before the South Carolina Supreme Court. He can then pursue state postconviction proceedings, which involve a hearing before a single judge (in J.C.'s case, Judge Peoples), followed by another appeal to the South Carolina Supreme Court. Finally, he can initiate a federal review of his case, beginning with the district court and then appealing to the circuit court of appeals. At the conclusion of each of these stages, a defendant's final resort is to petition the U.S. Supreme Court for certiorari, essentially asking the nation's highest court to consider the case and overrule the lower courts' decisions. Having exhausted his first two options, J.C.'s only hope lay with his federal appeals.

Dick Burr commenced J.C.'s federal court proceedings, refiling his supplemental petition for a writ of habeas corpus, as well as an amended petition in the district court. He also filed a motion seeking the recusal of Judge Hemphill, the district judge, based on his bias and prejudice stemming from his earlier involvement with J.C.'s case. It was Judge Hemphill who had denied J.C.'s request for a stay of execution on December 12, 1979, and who had found no basis for his claims of ineffective assistance of counsel, before even hearing his claim or seeing any of the evidence presented in support of it. After filing the motion, Dick Burr left the

Southern Prisoners' Defense Commission, which had since moved to Atlanta and was later renamed the Southern Center for Human Rights. Taking his place was Stephen Bright, a public defender from Washington, D.C, who had recently moved to Atlanta to serve as the commission's new director. Bright took over J.C.'s case in September 1982.

. . . .

The first impression Steve Bright had of his new client was his size. Already large at six feet three inches and weighing over two hundred pounds when he first arrived in prison, J.C. had put on an additional fifty pounds. "What a great big guy," Bright thought, shaking hands with him in the visiting room at CCI. Unlike other facilities he had visited, CCI allowed contact visits with its Death Row inmates, which meant he was able to confer with J.C. face-to-face. He already felt a unique affinity with him, having learned from Dick Burr that J.C., like Bright, was from Kentucky. J.C.'s reluctance to pursue his appeals had been put aside years ago. By the time Bright began to represent him, he was an eager and cooperative client.

Shortly after taking over the case, Bright argued the petition for a writ of habeas corpus in the district court before Judge Hemphill, who had refused to disqualify himself. Throughout the proceedings, Judge Hemphill made disparaging comments about J.C.'s case and his counsel, such as wondering aloud whether the Southern Center for Human Rights was a "subversive organization," describing the proceedings as a "maze of delay and departure from justice," and interrupting Bright's argument at one point to ask, "When did you think that one up?"

Bright got word just before Christmas that he had lost the case in the district court. He promptly called J.C. to report the outcome. Neither he nor J.C. was particularly surprised, having expected nothing more from Judge Hemphill. Instead, they tried to be optimistic about the appeal Bright planned to file in the U.S. Court of Appeals for the Fourth Circuit. At the time, it was considered a progressive circuit. After all, it was Judge Phillips from that very court who had granted J.C.'s stay in 1979. Bright's optimism also stemmed from the fact that the district court proceedings had been so egregiously bad and Judge Hemphill's conduct particularly outrageous. Surely even the most objective observer would agree that J.C. deserved another shot.

On Christmas day, Steve trudged into his office in downtown Atlanta to hammer out a petition for a rehearing. Before doing so, he reviewed the state's brief to the South Carolina Supreme Court in response to J.C.'s appeal of the denial of his postconviction relief. He was following up on a hunch he'd had when he had first read the order of summary judgement signed by Judge Hemphill. As he'd suspected, the two were practically identical. The bulk of Judge Hemphill's order was taken verbatim from the state's brief, including arguments and assessments of witnesses who were never presented before the court. Bright was outraged. At a minimum, J.C. was entitled to a fair and meaningful consideration of his case commensurate with the gravity of the issues presented. To supplant a judge's review with an advocate's brief was, he believed, a mockery of the justice system. He raised these issues in his petition for a rehearing, but Judge Hemphill did not agree with Bright's claims of unfairness, inaccuracy, and inappropriateness.

The appeal to the U.S. Court of Appeals for the Fourth Circuit, for which both J.C. and Bright had high hopes, was filed on November 7, 1983. The first argument set forth on J.C.'s behalf was that the district court's judgment should be reversed because of the bias and prejudice of the district court and Judge Hemphill's prejudgment of the issues before him. The second argument also involved Judge Hemphill, charging that he erred in denying an evidentiary hearing and in accepting the state court's finding.

The third argument, claiming that J.C.'s guilty pleas were constitutionally invalid, formed the basis of J.C.'s entitlement to federal habeas corpus relief. Bright first tried to establish that J.C. was not competent to make an independent, reasoned decision to waive his rights and plead guilty. In support of this claim, Bright argued that the trial court—despite having heard testimony that J.C. was suicidal and suffering from latent schizophrenia, alcoholism, drug abuse and emotional disorders—made no effort to determine the relationship between J.C.'s mental and emotional handicaps and his ability to make a knowing, voluntary, and intelligent plea. Judge Harwell had done very little probing in his assessment that J.C.'s plea was constitutionally sound. In fact, J.C.'s entire verbal exchange with the court consisted of the words, "Yes, Sir," "No, Sir," "twenty-two" (his age) and "tenth grade" (his educational level). Bright's second argument presented in support of the claim that J.C.'s guilty plea was invalid was the assertion that J.C. did not receive effective assistance of counsel regarding his decision to plead guilty. J.C.'s court-appointed counsel allowed him to plead guilty when he was incompetent to do so, failed to advise him of the trial judge's attitude regarding the death penalty, and induced him to plead guilty on patently erroneous legal advice.

Finally, Bright turned to the South Carolina Supreme Court's review of J.C.'s case, arguing that it failed to compare his case to similar cases to determine whether his sentence of death was disproportionate, in violation of the Eighth and Fourteenth Amendments. Since the Court could not find any cases similar to J.C.'s, it created a new category of cases starting with his. Bright concluded by requesting an oral argument for his appeal.

In April 1984, Bright argued the case before the U.S. Court of Appeals for the Fourth Circuit in Richmond, Virginia. His optimism remained intact throughout the proceedings. The court spent much of the time grilling the attorney general about how the lower courts had treated J.C., which made Bright feel confident that the judges saw things his way.

His surprise at the court's order denying J.C.'s appeal, entered shortly after the hearing on April 26, 1984, was surpassed only by his dismay. The panel's decision was unanimous; there was no dissent. Bright was in Alabama at the time teaching a continuing legal education course when he got word of the loss. He immediately called J.C. to break the news, not wanting him to hear it from the media first. Always candid with his clients, Bright told J.C. that losing this round meant big trouble. J.C. accepted the news stoically, remaining calm and asking what was next. Mary, whom Steve called next, exhibited none of her son's composure. She was devastated, and responded with sobs of anguish as soon as Bright told her the court had turned them down. Even though this was not the final step in J.C.'s appeals, no one held out much hope for the appeal Bright would file with the U.S. Supreme Court. They all appreciated it for the long shot it was.

. . . .

The maximum security unit at CCI comprises single cells in rows of cell blocks that face each other in a square. J.C.'s cell was in the second tier of Cell Block Two. His window faced the recreational yard outside, across from which he could see another cell block. His cell was nine feet long and six feet wide, allowing him to touch both walls with his arms outstretched. He had a bed with a plastic mattress and a sink with no running hot water. He was allowed out of his cell for a total of two hours per day, which could be spent interacting with other maximum security inmates in his cell block or undertaking Bible or legal study. As J.C. described it, "We get out to exercise three times per week for one hour each time. Our food is brought to us. I take a shower three times a week. Can't talk during the day because there would be too much noise, so the only time we talk is after 4:00, when the second shift comes."

J.C.'s day began with a holler for the count at 6:45 A.M. Each inmate would yell out his name, in turn, until all were accounted for. Breakfast was served at 7:00 A.M. and J.C. consumed it, like all meals, alone in his cell. Throughout the day, officers circulated to conduct surprise searches for contraband and to exercise their authority to ensure the inmates were getting along. Despite their efforts, fights frequently broke out whenever the inmates were out of their cells. Power plays among the different factions were a daily occurrence. The major part of the day was J.C.'s to do with as he wished, within the constraints of his solitary cell.

He spent most of his time reading a wide variety of books and magazines—whatever he could get from the prison library. His favorite novels were westerns and science fiction, and he liked news magazines. He was, by all accounts, a quiet and unobtrusive prisoner. He never posed any risk or created any disciplinary problems for the officers who patrolled his cell block.

The guards were not the only ones who appreciated J.C.'s even temper. By keeping to himself and never taking sides in the daily cell block disputes, J.C. also managed to win the respect of his fellow inmates. No matter which factions were in conflict, they always made a point of keeping J.C. out of it. Mary McFadden, a prison volunteer who had worked with more than 225 men on Death Row nationwide and more than 100 more in general prison populations, was particularly struck by J.C. "[He] soon became one of the most considerate, caring, unselfish, well-adjusted men I have worked with," she wrote to Governor Richard Riley prior to J.C.'s scheduled execution.

Outside visitors were allowed three times per week, but J.C. rarely used his allotted visitation time. His parents could not see him as frequently as they would have liked because of the expense and distance involved, but they spoke to him every Tuesday. In all of her jobs subsequent to J.C.'s incarceration, Mary always made a point of requesting Tuesday as her day off so that she would not miss J.C.'s calls. A surprisingly faithful visitor was

Ann Gibson, J.C.'s former mother-in-law. In her letter to the governor pleading for mercy, she said of J.C.: "I love him very much even as a son, and know him as the person he really is—A good caring boy, just a kid who found himself alone and out of reach of help . . ."

An important part of J.C.'s prison life was his written correspondence with his friends and family. Writing and receiving letters served as J.C.'s lifeline, albeit a frequently painful one, to the outside world.

June 21

Dear Dad,

It's a little late and sorta the wrong card but here it is. Frankie didn't get it to me in time, it was Friday when he brought it to me.

Nothin much going on here. All the kids out of school and running around now I guess. Dennis said Greg was getting pretty brave around him and thought he was top dog, so I guess Dennis is gonna bust him one if he keeps it up. Ha ha.

Haven't heard nothing from the lawyer's. I think Pat Toathy is supposed to come down the month.

Well, guess I'll go, "Happy Fathers Day"

Love, J.C.

Aug. 14

Dear Dennis,

I'm just getting back to you on your letter, got a few things to write about. Tell mom I'm not sure when I'll get to call again, the phone people are on strike and the people here are using that as an excuse for not letting us make calls. Next time you talk to Debbie and Robert tell them Happy Birthday for me. Glad to here about your grade's, your doing great—not to bad with the girls either huh!

This picture was in the TV Guide it's where I live. You can make out a little bit, it's home sweet home.

Well school starts soon, is that good or bad. I guess you set around all summer doing nothing, that's about all I ever did with my summer's. It's cooled down her a little bit, in the low 90's.

Well I guess I'll go, take care and say hi to everybody for me.

Stay chilly,

Love, J.C.

Through his letters, J.C. managed to maintain a presence in his younger brothers' lives as they went through adolescence and young adulthood. Pat Murray, a family friend, viewed J.C.'s relationship with Robert Jr., Dennis, and Greg as instrumental in J.C.'s rehabilitation. "He remains close with [them]," she wrote in support of J.C.'s clemency petition, "and, as is expected of older brothers, often dishes out the brotherly advice, 'speaking from experience.' It is a difficult relationship to maintain long-distance, but they do it and do it well."

> *Dear Robert,*
>
> *How are you doing? Mom said you and Robin have broken up. I hope it's not for good. I just wanted to write and see if your ok. When I broke up with Karyn things didn't go to good with me, so I want to make sure you don't wind up like me. If you need to talk about it I hope you will write me and let me know. I never talked to anybody when I broke up and after awhile it got to be to much for me to handle and so here I am. I hope you don't have to go through all that, so if you need to talk about it write me ok?*
>
> *I'll be here if you need me.*
>
> > *Take care.*
> >
> > *Love, J.C.*

In addition to dispensing advice, J.C. also clipped articles of interest to send to his brothers. He once sent an article on astronomy to Dennis, who was a science buff and the only strong student among the brothers, noting, "I don't get this stuff, but I know you find it interesting so I cut it out for you."

J.C. also struck up "pen pal" relationships with strangers who wrote to him, including a teenage boy in St. Louis, with whom he exchanged letters for three and a half years. A few days prior to his scheduled execution, J.C. received a letter from the boy's mother thanking him for bringing joy into her son's life. Reflecting on his unique relationship with the St. Louis teen, J.C. concluded, "He was pretty much like me. I don't communicate with my friends that much. If I had problems, I kept them to myself so I think that's basically what he did."

. . . .

Jim Aiken tried to relax as he headed east on Interstate 20 toward Myrtle Beach, South Carolina. It was a beautiful October morning in 1984, and he was on his way to a meeting with other wardens of state penitentiaries. Even though this was a work trip, it felt good to get away. In addition to the daily challenges and inevitable problems associated with running a prison, the work also took an emotional toll on Aiken. Having started his correctional career as a psychiatric social worker, Jim cared more than most wardens about his prison and the convicts it housed.

Most of the inmates on Death Row had rap sheets as long as their burly arms, stemming from a life of crime and misadventures. The cell blocks in which they lived required constant surveillance, since most of them posed a security risk and committed numerous infractions. Every once in a while, however, there was an exception—that rare inmate with whom Aiken could truly identify and sympathize. J.C. Shaw was such a prisoner.

J.C. had already been on Death Row for several years when Aiken took over as CCI's warden in 1982. Right from the start, J.C. struck Aiken as a step above his fellow inmates, someone who did not at all fit the profile of what he had done. Unusually quiet and meek, J.C. followed all the prison rules and regulations while maintaining the respect and friendship of his fellow inmates. Aiken sympathized with J.C., often wondering what it must be like to spend every day regretting the actions you took on two particular days.

Making a conscious effort to try to focus on issues unrelated to the prison, Aiken turned on the radio. As soon as the news came on, Aiken's thoughts instantly returned to J.C. The newscaster stated that the U.S. Supreme Court had finished its session and rendered several rulings, some of which involved denials of certiorari for several death penalty cases. Jim knew J.C.'s case had to be among those mentioned. As soon as he arrived at Myrtle Beach, he called CCI's legal office, which confirmed that the Supreme Court had, in fact, declined to review J.C.'s case.

When Aiken returned to CCI, he did not see the changes he expected J.C. to exhibit in his behavior. He had seen many inmates become extremely antisocial and combative once their final appeals were turned down, probably feeling that they no longer had anything to lose. To Aiken, this proved that J.C.'s calm and cooperative demeanor was not an act. That brief period of time when he committed those heinous crimes was an anomaly; it did not define his personality.

. . . .

> *Dear Governor,*
>
> *This is concerning J.C. Shaw. I am J.C.'s youngest brother. I am 17 years old. I was about 10 when this all happened. We look up to him like a father. I know for a fact that he would not have done what he did if he was sane at the time. He got into drugs which really messed up his head. All I want is for him to live. I know if he dies, so will my mom. Please commute his sentence for our family and the people who love him. If it happens, they will be killing more than one man.*
>
> *Pray to God when you make your decision.*
>
> *Gregory Crum*

On December 18, 1984, the "Application of Joseph Carl Shaw for Commutation of Sentence of Death" was submitted to the Honorable Richard W. Riley, the governor of South Carolina at that time and currently the secretary of education in the Clinton Administration. Even though the clemency petition represents the absolute last hope a Death Row inmate has of avoiding execution, J.C. and his supporters were hopeful about his prospects. The petition was filled with testimonials from over fifty-eight people, who all knew J.C. at different periods of his life, including several who had come to know him only during his incarceration. All begged the governor to spare his life.

As Bright stated at the outset,

> **Neither counsel, Joseph Carl Shaw, nor his family assert that he is not responsible for the homicides which occurred. Nor do we question that severe punishment is required. We address in this application only the question of whether a number of compelling factors justify use of your power as Governor to intervene and prevent infliction of the ultimate punishment of death upon our client.**

The letter from Bruce Pearson, a volunteer teacher at CCI, tried to balance J.C.'s crimes against the rest of his life:

> **If J.C. is put to death at this point, it will be necessary to kill not only the person who was out of control for a few months in 1977, but along with him the one time altar boy, the unexceptional student and the good soldier who inhabited his body until 1977, and of course the model prisoner who has taken his place since late 1977.**

J.C. was initially optimistic about how his clemency petition would be received. He hoped the strength of his particular case and the governor's views on the death penalty would lead the governor to the right decision. After all, when Governor Riley was a state senator, he voted against the death penalty in the legislature, based on his convictions of Christian conscience.

On Thursday, December 20, 1984, Aiken received a call from CCI's legal office informing him that the South Carolina Supreme Court had issued a death warrant for J.C. He then had the unpleasant task of summoning J.C. to his office so that he could read it to him. The warrant stated that all of J.C.'s appeals were denied and that it was the court's order that he be executed on the fourth Friday after receipt of the warrant. Since the very next day counted as the first Friday, J.C. was essentially given three weeks to live. The execution was officially scheduled for Friday, January 11, 1985. J.C. took the news stoically, but he was clearly nervous and flustered.

Pursuant to the prison's policy, Aiken asked J.C. what he wanted done with respect to the disposition of his body.

"I don't know," J.C. stammered. "I haven't thought about that yet."

"What about the disposition of your personal belongings?" Aiken asked.

"Give them to Steve," J.C. responded. "He'll take care of everything."

. . . .

The Crum family traveled to Columbia, filled with the sickening sense that this would be their last trip. Greg opted not to go, a decision that did not sit well with his mother. She wanted to force him to accompany the family, convinced he was simply staying behind because he wanted to spend time with his girlfriend. Robert Sr., who prevailed in the end, felt strongly that they shouldn't force the boys to go. Besides, he did not share Mary's view that Greg's reluctance was unconnected to J.C. and the execution. He knew Greg was struggling with his brother's impending death, even though he had never articulated his angst. Dennis agreed to go, but made it clear he would need to return home before the execution in order to register for courses at the University of Louisville. Robert Sr. knew this was just an excuse, particularly when he later learned that Dennis didn't register until many weeks later, but he respected the fact that Dennis knew his own limits. In the end, Robert Sr. and Mary were joined only by Robert Jr.

It was Christmastime, but no one was feeling remotely festive. On

Thursday, January 2, 1985, J.C. was transferred from CCI's Death Row to the Capital Punishment Facility (CPF), more commonly referred to as the Death House. Following the prison's protocol, referred to for the first time in over twenty years, J.C. was officially photographed and fingerprinted. He was also given new prison garb, since he was now officially a Department of Corrections inmate rather than an inmate of the county.

The Crums divided their time between visiting J.C. and trying to get Governor Riley to meet with them and hear their pleas for mercy. "Everyone has painted J.C. as an animal," Robert Jr. told reporters when he made his family's appeal to the governor public. "If Governor Riley would only meet with him, I just know he wouldn't kill him." The governor ultimately designated certain members of his staff to serve as advisors and conduct the inquiry, but he refused to meet with J.C. himself.

It was clear to Steve Bright that Governor Riley was insulating himself from J.C. and had no intention of meeting with him or getting personally involved in his case. A sentencing hearing is awkward enough when one looks directly at the person who is being sentenced to death. A clemency hearing, however, is even more intense. J.C.'s death was no longer an abstract, future event but something that was scheduled to take place in a matter of days. The advisors, who all shook hands and spoke with J.C., could not help being moved. Bright had no way of knowing what they ultimately advised the governor to do, but he became increasingly convinced that the governor's decision had been made irrespective of their recommendation.

In direct contrast to the lack of cooperation and sympathy exhibited by Governor Riley, the prison's accommodation of J.C.'s family could not have been more generous. Visiting hours were extended, and the guards who were posted in the Death House to keep J.C. under constant surveillance were extremely cordial and helpful.

The first day the family trudged into J.C.'s cell, the entire visit was spent crying and consoling each other. Once they ran out of things to say, they all sat and stared at each other or at the floor in an awkward silence. The next day, J.C. greeted them with a deck of cards and the admonition that he did not want a repeat of the previous day's visit. He wanted their time together to be festive and fun. His family was dubious at first, but in no time they were all laughing and carrying on together. Mary worried about what the guard would think, but when she caught his eye, he winked and nodded his approval. The remainder of their days together were spent playing poker or Trivial Pursuit. Mary still has the deck of cards and the bag of dimes and nickels they used as a memento of their final family gathering.

. . . .

In his final days, J.C. was the subject of quite a media blitz. The notoriety of his crimes coupled with the fact that this was the first execution in South Carolina in twenty-two years captured the public's attention. Death penalty fervor was so high that a local businessman quickly sold the one thousand bumper stickers he had printed, illustrated with the electric chair and the words "Use it." A local TV station was flooded with calls from viewers who were under the impression the execution would be televised live.

J.C. also gave a few interviews. Asked if he thought the death penalty was a deterrent, he said: "If anything, I think it raises crime a little bit. Because the state is saying it's okay to kill because we are going to go ahead and show you by doing it." Asked what he would say to the victims' families if given the chance, he responded: "I'd just say I am very sorry that this happened and I wish there were something I could do about it. If dying on Friday would bring them back, then I'd go ahead and tell them to move the date up to today." With respect to his feelings about the actual execution, he stated: "I won't be screaming and fighting or anything. The penalty—I've accepted it and I know I'll go with the help of the Lord." He added that he wasn't worried about dying, but "it's the thought of leaving my family and friends, and how my mother, father, and brothers are going to feel after I am gone."

He also commented on the crimes themselves and his thoughts about what he had done.

> Another personality—an animal—killed three people in 1977 and the real Shaw stood back and watched, as if in a movie. I still hear voices and see visions, but the voices don't tell me to do those bad things anymore. They remind me what I did to those people and I see it happening all over again. It still feels like it was somebody else, not me, but I take the responsibility. I bear the blame. I know I'm going to die and I know it's happening to me, except J.C. Shaw, the way I am today, is not going to die. The animal that I was then is going to die.

. . . .

On Thursday, January 10, the entire atmosphere changed. The previous days' frivolity was gone, replaced with a solemnity and sadness that pervaded the entire Death House and everyone associated with it. The visitors in J.C.'s cell were somber and quiet, having nothing to say to each other but needing nonetheless to be together. At noon, everyone trudged out to get some lunch and some much-needed air—everyone but Robert Jr., who chose to stay behind and remain with his big brother.

At first, he and J.C. simply sat facing each other, not saying anything.

"I reckon we're going to need this," J.C. said, tossing Robert a roll of toilet paper.

Both men began to cry, the kind of crying they'd needed to do for a long time. They also talked, the kind of talking they had been unable to do with everyone else around.

"I want so bad for this not to happen," J.C. said again and again. It was the only time he let anyone see his fear and despair about his impending death.

When the rest of the family came back from lunch, J.C. returned to his role of providing comfort and courage. They all shared J.C.'s final meal of pizza, tossed salad, and soda. At 11:00 P.M., Steve Bright quietly but firmly indicated to the Crums that it was time for them to leave. The guard's hands shook as he locked the cell door separating J.C. from his departing family.

Before they exited the Death House, the Crums turned around for one final glimpse of J.C. through the glass partition. J.C. lifted up his arms, which were handcuffed together at the wrists, and made a thumbs up gesture. He then smiled at his family, giving them the strength to turn and leave. As they walked outside, numb with the knowledge that J.C. would be dead by daylight, Robert Jr. heard the deputy warden mutter, "Here we finally rehabilitate one, and then we kill him."

. . . .

Jim Aiken relinquished total authority for running CCI to his deputy warden. Aiken's sole focus and responsibility was to carry out South Carolina's first execution in twenty-two years. He assigned his senior deputy warden to take care of J.C.'s family and any issues related to their visit.

To another officer he assigned the role of dealing with the media circus that had developed outside of his office. The one responsibility that he could not delegate was oversight of the execution itself. In the weeks preceding the execution, Aiken and his staff quietly practiced the execution in the Death House, knowing that J.C. was in a cell just a few feet away.

As far as his job was concerned, it didn't matter what Aiken's personal views on the death penalty were or how he felt about J.C. His role was to ensure that the sentence of the state versus Joseph Carl Shaw was carried out on January 11, 1985. In the final week, Aiken found it impossible to think of anything else. Even if he could have put thoughts of J.C. and the execution aside, the media and public would not have let him. He was bombarded with calls—reporters wanting to get an exclusive interview, fanatics wanting to witness the execution, family and friends concerned about J.C. or simply curious.

By noon on Thursday, Aiken was totally numb. He was operating on remote control, focusing exclusively on the task at hand. He watched the family come and go, and struggled not to dwell on what this must be like for them. Steve Bright and Father Duffy were told they could stay as long as they wished; both remained with J.C. all night.

Midnight marked the start of the final preparations. Jim kept checking to make sure that the direct phone lines to the governor and the attorney general were in working order. They worked, but they weren't ringing. Electricians set to work checking the system and its backups. Aiken and the guards on duty reviewed the extensive security procedures.

The gravity of what he was preparing to do was overwhelming Aiken. All the rhetoric was rendered meaningless. "I'm taking someone's life," he kept marveling to himself. J.C., sensing Aiken's distress, told him he did not blame him.

"You're just doing your job," J.C. said. "I don't hold you responsible."

. . . .

In the final hours, Bright and J.C. were alone. Sleep was out of the question. J.C. made some calls, talking to family members back home and to Gerry Spence. He was very much concerned about how his family was holding up, and made Bright promise he would call them as soon as it was all over. He also worked on his final statement, enlisting Bright's help in writing it out on a yellow legal pad.

First, I want to say I am sorry to all three families—the Swanks, the Taylors and the Hartnesses—for the grief and loss they have suffered. I realize their grief will continue, but I hope they have some peace once all the publicity about me ends.

I also want to say thanks to my mother, father and other family members and friends who have stood beside me for seven long, hard years. I also want to thank all those who wrote letters for me to Gov. Riley and the many people who have remembered me in their prayers.

To Archbishop Kelly of Louisville, thanks for the support of my family and your strong voice against the death penalty. To Monsignor Duffy, Frankie-San and the others who have given me religious counseling, I express my deepest thanks. I am able to die in peace with the strength of faith thanks to them. I am proud that my church, the Roman Catholic Church, and his Holiness, Pope John Paul II, have stood strongly for human life and against the death penalty.

To my lawyers, Steve Bright, Dick Burr, Ken Suggs, John Delgado and Gerry Spence, and the other lawyers, students and staff who worked with them, thanks for many hard-fought legal battles. If I had you at the start, I would not be here today.

To those who oppose the death penalty in South Carolina and the many who attended last night's service, I say continue the fight against the hatred, vengeance and revenge of this primitive form of punishment.

To the other guys on Death Row, I say stay strong and keep up the fight.

To all those who have sought my death and to Gov. Riley, I hope you learn by your mistake. Killing was wrong when I did it. It is wrong when you do it. I hope you have the courage and the moral strength to stop the killing. I have no bitterness toward anyone. May God bless and forgive you all.

The hours between midnight and 4:00 A.M. went by in slow motion. Once the final preparations began, however, the pace picked up considerably. The first order of business was to shave J.C.'s head, which took a while since his hair had grown quite long. The care the officers took struck Father Duffy as painfully ironic.

"They're being so careful not to nick him," he muttered to Bright. "And in just a few minutes, they're going to electrocute him."

J.C. also found humor in the situation. He jokingly said to Bright, in reference to his newly shaved head, "If Governor Riley pardons me now, I'll kill him."

They also shaved J.C.'s right leg from ankle to knee. At 4:15 A.M., J.C. showered and dressed in a clean, light blue shirt and dark blue denim pants. The right pant leg was split to make room for the electrodes. J.C. was then escorted by two officers to the electrocution chamber, where he was forcefully and dramatically strapped into the electric chair. Aiken asked J.C. if he wanted to say anything. J.C. nodded. He was too shaky to hold his statement himself, however, so Bright held it up for him as he read it.

After J.C. read his statement, Father Duffy, clutching a small green Bible, administered a blessing. He then patted J.C. on the arm and stepped back, making room for Bright's farewell.

"I love you, J.C.," Bright whispered to him, then bent down and kissed him on the right cheek.

Bright and Father Duffy left the death chamber together, both red-eyed and quiet. They then turned and watched what they had hoped never to see.

A tan leather strap was placed across J.C.'s mouth, tying his head back against the chair. A black leather cap was then placed on his head, over which a brown hood was lowered to cover his face. An electrode was secured around J.C.'s ankle and a black wire from the chair was attached to the black cap on his head.

At 5:07 A.M., Aiken signaled to the three volunteer executioners, who were hidden behind a partition with their hands positioned over the electrical switches. None of the three knew which ones were the two dummies and which one was the active executioner, so that they were spared the knowledge of which of them had administered the fatal shocks.

Harvey Burgess, one of two newsmen who were allowed to witness and report on the execution, described what happened next:

> **In about a minute, Shaw's 260-pound frame lurched abruptly against the restraints on the chair, causing a flapping noise. His body convulsed eight times, then remained rigid, his fists clenched, for about a minute.**
>
> **Thin wisps of what appeared to be smoke rose from the rolled-up pants leg.**

After the first jolt of electricity, Shaw's body relaxed against the chair about 10 seconds and the second jolt stiffened his body again, though the second convulsion was less pronounced than the first.

A minute later, Shaw's body relaxed again, slowly sinking back into the chair.

After a two-minute pause, the white-clad medical technician—a large, bearded man—walked up to Shaw's body, gripped Shaw's left wrist in his left hand and placed his right hand against Shaw's neck.

The technician held his hands in place for about three minutes, then, using a stethoscope, listened to Shaw's heart.

He looked over at the doctor, nodded his head, and returned to his chair while the doctor walked up, checked Shaw's wrist and neck, then placed his stethoscope inside Shaw's T-shirt to listen for a heartbeat.

The doctor lifted the hood slightly and, using a pen-sized flashlight, apparently examined Shaw's eyes. Then he looked at Aiken and nodded.

Aiken picked up the microphone.

"The sentence of the State versus Joseph Carl Shaw has been carried out," he said.

. . . .

It was hard enough dealing with J.C.'s death without the additional burden of having to do so under so much public scrutiny. The Crums were besieged with interview requests after the execution, and TV cameras followed them around everywhere. They held a lot of press conferences, but felt acutely uncomfortable being in the spotlight.

"We're just poor folks from Kentucky," Robert Sr. mused. "We're out of our element."

The calls from reporters continued for a long time afterward. The Crums also received several death threats and anonymous calls. For six months following the execution, Mary refused to leave the house. She didn't want to risk anyone talking to her about J.C. Robert Sr. had to contend not only with Mary's depression, but with his own despair. He was haunted by an interview J.C. had given prior to the execution, in which he said that if he could erase the events of 1977 and be free, he'd go back to Kentucky and do construction work with his stepfather again. "I was happy there," J.C. said. "And I was never in trouble there."

The family buried J.C. at Floydsburg Cemetery in Crestwood, Kentucky. The following year, when they took Steve Bright there to visit J.C.'s grave, Bright recognized the adjacent chapel as the one in which he had been married many years before. The coincidence served to underscore Bright's link to J.C., somehow completing the circle of their relationship.

donald wayne thomas

> "John seems ready. He seems at peace. In some way I think
> that he's relieved [the Warden said]. I appreciate your profes-
> sional attitude through all this."
>
> I thanked him too. I thanked him for his professional attitude
> and his courtesy. I thanked him for making it easier for John and
> his family. We shook hands.
>
> I had to wonder at our roles. We were professionals. He was
> the executioner and I was the defense lawyer. Here we were
> thanking each other for being so professional. One pro to an-
> other. For doing what? Making a hard job more bearable? For
> helping reduce tensions all around? For making it go down
> easier?
>
> Damn, I thought. This man is going to kill John in about
> three hours. He is going to pull the switch and shoot electricity
> through John's head and fry his brains out. That's exactly what
> he's going to do.
>
> And here I am thanking him for being a pro. What was I doing
> in all this? Another pro. A respectable cog in this grotesque ma-
> chinery of butchery. My job was to help provide a clean execu-
> tion. I should be screaming and shouting. I should make them
> drag me out of there—create a scene. I should make it as hard
> and tough and as sick and inhumane as it was. I should be mak-
> ing my voice heard in this ritual of cruelty. I should make these
> bastards hear my voice and know what the hell they are doing.

Russell F. Canan, writing about the 1984 execution of his client, John
Evans, is now an associate judge on the Superior Court of the District of
Columbia. At the time of Evans's execution, Canan was one of three attorneys who had joined Stephen Bright in Atlanta to represent Death Row
prisoners at the Southern Prisoners' Defense Commission. His cynicism
about his role as a capital defender and his disgust with the legal system
that rendered many of his efforts futile were a far cry from the optimism
and hope with which he embraced his first capital case, that of Donald
Wayne Thomas.

In 1976, Canan and two fellow graduates of Antioch Law School established the law firm of Canan, Burns, and O'Toole in Washington, D.C.
The firm's mission was to defend the city's indigent, and its practice consisted exclusively of court-appointed criminal defense work. In 1977,
George Kendall joined the law firm, having worked there as a law clerk

while pursuing his law degree at Antioch. Canan and Steve Bright met when they were appointed to represent codefendents in a murder trial. By the time the trial was over, they had both tried their first murder case and had forged a close friendship. Kendall, who had limited trial experience at the time, often sought advice from Bright, who had already established a reputation as a brilliant defense attorney at the District's Public Defender Service (PDS).

By 1980, Bright had left PDS to run a legal clinic called Law Students in Court. He remained committed to criminal defense work, however, and was particularly interested in pursuing capital cases. Horrified by the U.S. Supreme Court's 1976 reinstatement of the death penalty, Canan and Kendall shared Bright's interest in representing Death Row defendants. It was their common desire to get involved in the growing anti–death penalty movement that prompted all three men to attend a speech at Washington's All Souls Church given by Millard Farmer, a renowned anti–death penalty crusader from Atlanta, Georgia.

Bright, Canan, and Kendall listened as Farmer described defendants who were sentenced to death but had no one to represent them. "This just can't be right," Kendall thought. "Surely if a state has the death penalty, it will ensure that each defendant is represented."

By the end of the talk, which culminated with a plea for volunteers, Kendall was eager to help. He arranged to have lunch with David Kendall (no relation), an attorney at the Washington law firm of Williams and Connelly, who was screening legal volunteers at Farmer's behest.

Two weeks later, Patsy Morris called him. Morris, a volunteer with the Georgia chapter of the American Civil Liberties Union (ACLU), was singlehandedly responsible for matching unrepresented Death Row defendants in Georgia with volunteer legal counsel across the country.

"I understand you're willing to take on a capital case," she said. "I have a Georgia case that needs to have a cert. petition [requesting that the U.S. Supreme Court review the case] filed in sixty days. Can you do it?"

Kendall's response was anything but a resounding yes. Despite his desire to get involved, he knew that a capital case would require significant time and resources. Wading through the record, let alone researching and writing the cert. petition, would undoubtedly consume the entire summer. He told Morris he would have to check with Canan and get back to her.

"Let's do it," Canan said when Kendall approached him about it. "But let's get Steve in on it with us." After Bright agreed, Kendall called Morris back. He told her to go ahead and send him the record for Donald (Donny) Wayne Thomas.

. . . .

The record that Kendall, Canan, and Bright all anticipated would arrive in a U-Haul truck arrived instead in a simple manila envelope. What Kendall had feared would take an entire summer to read was no more than an inch and a half thick and took him but one night to digest.

"This is it?" Canan exclaimed incredulously when he saw it.

As they read through the shockingly short transcript of the trial, Kendall, Bright, and Canan found there was hardly any participation in the trial by Donny's only court-appointed attorney, Robert Coker.

The size of the record was particularly jarring to Bright because he had always assumed that no one would get the death penalty without elaborate measures taken on his behalf. Donny's meager court papers served as a rude reminder of how poorly capital cases could be tried. The eleven-page brief to Georgia's Supreme Court appealing Donny's sentence of death was so limited in its scope and length that Bright was convinced it would not have received a passing grade in a first-year law school class. Even more shocking was the fact that a court had decided the case on that limited basis. Kendall was equally stunned by the fact that the judicial system had treated an individual whose life was at stake in such a perfunctory way.

The trial transcript revealed a trial so mechanical that it appeared Robert Coker, a local public defender, had done little more than show up. There were no pretrial motions, no discovery, an alarmingly brief opening statement (taking up one and a half pages of transcript compared to the customary forty to fifty pages) and no evidence whatsoever presented at the penalty phase.

"Students in my clinic try shoplifting cases better than this," Bright muttered in disgust.

But the meager defense mounted on Donny's behalf was not the only jarring aspect of his record. The state's case was equally shocking in its sketchiness. Kendall, Bright, and Canan had simply assumed that the incriminating evidence in a capital case would have to be overwhelming in order to convict someone and sentence him to death. But one reading of the record in Donny's case left all three men feeling significant doubts about his guilt. The state's case seemed to focus primarily on the accusations of two witnesses: Linda Cook, Donny's live-in girlfriend at the time of the crime, and Enzer Lowe, Donny's stepfather. Cook was a fifteen-year-old, mildly retarded girl; Lowe was an alcoholic who later recanted his testimony, claiming he was drunk and high at the time.

It was also clear from the record that Donny's mental health was questionable at best, but there had not been a competency hearing. Nor was any evidence presented at his trial or at his sentencing about his mental capacity at the time of the crime and at the trial. Donny was examined by two psychiatrists, both selected by the court, who provided conflicting reports as to his mental state. The first psychiatrist found that Donny was mentally incompetent to stand trial. The court then sought a second opinion from another psychiatrist, who did not reach an opinion and recommended that Donny be examined by the state hospital. After examining Donny for one month, the doctors at the state hospital reported to the court that Donny was competent to stand trial despite the fact that he suffered from "latent schizophrenia." The court never held a hearing to obtain opinions from any of the doctors who examined Donny, even though Donny was unable to effectively communicate with his attorney and sat throughout the trial with his clenched fist raised in some kind of salute.

Donny's newly appointed attorneys knew they had their work cut out for them, since they had never filed a cert. petition before, nor had they handled any other aspects of a capital case. Nevertheless, they felt sure that Donny's death sentence could not stand because of his mental limitations and the shoddy representation he had received.

. . . .

On April 11, 1979, Dewey Baugus and a playmate went to a ball game together. After the game, the two nine-year-old boys separated to return to their respective homes in the early evening darkness. Baugus, who was white, lived with his mother in a predominantly black neighborhood on Primrose Circle, in Atlanta. His playmate was the last person to see him alive.

Baugus was found one week later, lying face down on the railroad tracks behind Primrose Circle. He had been brutally strangled to death, and his pants were pulled down to midthigh level. The autopsy report showed numerous postmortem bruises and lacerations.

Donald Wayne Thomas, a nineteen-year-old black man, lived in a rooming house on Primrose Circle. He had dropped out of high school by the tenth grade, having learned little more than how to read and write his own name. He left his mother's house as soon as he could support himself, which he did by working as a dishwasher at Grandma's Biscuits Restaurant in Doraville, Georgia, where he was a valued employee. Each morning he would rise at 3:00 A.M. and take two buses across town to the restaurant, where his shift started at 4:00 A.M. Frances Long, a manager of Grandma's Biscuits Restaurant, later testified that Donny was one of the hardest-working and the most dependable employees of the hundreds she had supervised over the years. He compensated for his limited intelligence and schooling with his diligence and determination. Once he was shown a new task, he would practice it until he had mastered it. Donny was such a trusted employee that Long hired him to do yard work at her residence.

Donny never knew his father. His mother, an alcoholic, opened her doors to a succession of men until she married Enzer Lowe when Donny was sixteen. "I was raised properly," Donny said twenty years later of his childhood. "My Mama didn't put nothin' but love in me." He acknowledges, however, that both his mother and stepfather drank heavily, and that they became hostile and violent whenever they were drunk. After dodging a few too many bottles and fists, Donny moved into the rooming house.

As noted earlier, Linda Cook, his fifteen-year-old, mildly retarded girlfriend, lived with him. Like most of the men in his neighborhood, Donny believed in keeping a woman in her place. He was a man, so he got to call the shots. Also at play in his treatment of Cook, however, was Donny's undiagnosed schizophrenia, which typically surfaces during a person's late teens or early twenties and skewed Donny's perception of reality.

As described in the 1991 book *Psychiatric Disorders in America* (edited by Lee N. Robins and Darrell A. Pegier [New York: Free Press]) schizophrenia "alters the expectations of . . . two to four million people [in the United States] at just the time when those affected may be trying to complete an education or select a career." The course of the illness is unrelenting for approximately one third of those who suffer from it, while "[f]or an additional 50% disabling symptoms are expected to appear intermittently throughout life, spawning further social and occupational disabilities."

Even when treatment is sought and provided, it "frequently fail[s] to provide protection from the pattern of repeated relapse and functional decline that is a clinical hallmark of the illness."

In the week before Cook turned Donny in to the authorities, she had been locked up in his room while he was out.

"I didn't trust her to stay put and not mess around behind my back," Donny says, rationalizing what struck him as a logical means of keeping her in line. Without acknowledging the inappropriateness of his approach, he now appreciates that imprisoning Cook made for an irate and vengeful girlfriend.

Cook told the police that when Donny returned to the room on April 13, she noticed that he had a lot of blood on the front of his pants. She said that Donny then took her to the railroad tracks behind Primrose Circle and showed her the body of a little boy lying face down and told her that he had killed the child by beating him with a stick and choking him. According to the trial court's subsequent findings,

> [i]n her presence, the appellant [Donny] rolled the body over. Telling her that he had to make sure that he was dead, the appellant then jumped on the neck of the victim. Thereafter, he threw the victim's body in the bushes. Thereafter, they returned to the room, where the appellant removed his pants and hid them behind the house. That same day, the appellant, again in Linda Cook's presence, admitted the murder to his stepfather, Enzer Lowe. However, the stepfather testified that he did not believe him because the appellant was grinning about it.

Since Cook did not apprise the police of the crime for several days, she was charged with concealing a death and placed in juvenile detention. She remained incarcerated for the six months preceding the trial. In exchange for her testimony at Donny's trial, Cook was given immunity from prosecution. Donny's discarded pants were recovered, and crime lab tests confirmed that the blood on them was human, International Type B. However, lab technicians were unable to determine whether the blood matched that of the victim, since Baugus's body was too decayed for his blood type to be established.

When confronted with the evidence against him, Donny protested his innocence, and he has continued to do so to this day. He said he was not concerned initially about his predicament because he knew he hadn't committed the crime in question. His credibility, already questionable given his role as the sole suspect in the case, was rendered even more suspect because of his criminal record. Donny already had prior convictions for child molestation and assault with intent to rape, enabling not only the police, but also the court and the jury, to perceive him as capable of Baugus's murder. Donny claims his troubling convictions stemmed from a foiled robbery attempt of a house where there were two six-year-old girls. He says he was not even with his friends when the crime was committed, but he "copped a plea for zip to six" because he viewed a conviction as inevitable and thought a plea would at least allow him to obtain some medications he could not otherwise afford.

Donny never made any statement to law enforcement authorities about Baugus's murder, nor did he testify at trial. He was convicted on the basis of Linda Cook's and Enzer Lowe's testimony and the circumstantial evidence of his bloody pants. On October 24, 1979, a jury of the Superior Court of Fulton County, Georgia, found Donny guilty of murder. It found the statutory aggravating circumstance "that the strangling of a nine-year-old child was outrageously and wantonly vile, horrible and inhuman in that it involved torture and depravity of mind" and sentenced him to death.

. . . .

Donny was represented at trial by Robert Coker, the Fulton County public defender who was appointed to represent him on May 14, 1979—nearly one month after Donny's arrest. Coker met with Donny on only ten occasions prior to his trial in October. Each visit took place at the jail and lasted only a short time. Donny did not perceive Coker as being on his side, and eventually ceased communicating with him altogether.

"He didn't do nothin' to investigate the case or talk to folks," Donny recalls angrily.

Describing his visits with his client, Coker testified that Donny "would sit in his part of the visiting room and rock back and forth and would not communicate with me." Noting that Donny was "experiencing significant difficulty in communicating coherently," Coker moved for a psychiatric examination. The trial court appointed Dr. Lloyd Baccus of Grady Hospital, who examined Donny and reported that he was incompetent. Dr. Baccus's findings were based on the fact that during the examination, Donny "became increasingly restless and agitated, eventually ceasing to respond to questions while rocking back and forth in the chair and rubbing his genitals with his hands." Dr. Baccus also concluded that Donny had symptoms "clearly indicative of a diagnosis of schizophrenia" and that he was "so substantially impaired . . . as to be unable to assist his attorney in the preparation and implementation of his defense."

The court then solicited a second opinion, that of Dr. Sheldon Cohen, who was "unable to make a definite diagnosis or state an opinion" as to Donny's competency to stand trial. Since his findings were inconclusive, Dr. Cohen recommended that Donny be evaluated in an institutional setting. Pursuant to court order, Donny was subsequently sent to Central State Hospital, in Milledgeville, Georgia, for an inpatient evaluation.

When he entered Central State, Donny was again observed "rocking in his chair, anxious, occasionally putting his hands on his genitals, having gross tremors of his legs, and unable to provide good information about his birth and early development." After examining Donny for one month, the hospital doctors prepared a written report for the court, stating that their tests suggested thought disorders resembling a schizophrenic process, but expressing the opinion that Donny was competent to stand trial.

Coker initially sought to pursue an insanity defense, but Dr. Baccus informed him that he did not think there was a basis for presenting such a defense. As was later pointed out by the court on appeal, Coker

> **never sought to employ his own psychiatrist or any other mental health professional to assist him with making his own evaluation and judgment as to Mr. Thomas' state of mind. He never contacted either Dr. Cohen or anyone at Central State Hospital to inquire as to the scope of their evaluations or to determine by what process they had arrived at their opinions. He therefore had no way of knowing, at the beginning of the trial, whether the Central State opinion declaring Mr. Thomas competent was reliable or was totally inaccurate.**

Coker abandoned any further review of Donny's competency to stand trial or his mental state during the trial, despite the fact that Donny's behavior remained abnormal. Donny did not communicate with Coker during most of the trial, sitting instead at counsel table with one hand held in the air in what is commonly understood to be a "black power" salute. Coker was unable to persuade Donny to refrain from this inappropriate behavior.

Coker concluded that the only defense available to him was to challenge the credibility of the state's two key witnesses. It never occurred to him, however, to challenge their competency. Linda Cook had substantial mental limitations and had been incarcerated for the previous six months, and Enzer Lowe had a chronic drinking problem that could explain why he did not believe Donny's story. At the state habeas hearing, Lowe informed the court that he testified falsely at trial because he "had been jailed right before trial, was suffering from withdrawal from alcohol, and was afraid."

Coker's opening statement at the beginning of the trial should have instantly called the jury's attention to the fact that the state's case had numerous holes and depended on unreliable witnesses. Instead, Coker simply introduced himself and asked the jury to keep an open mind. His trial strategy, as he later disclosed, was to rely on Donny and his mother to testify on Donny's behalf. Donny steadfastedly refused to testify at any phase of the trial and told Coker that he did not want anyone else "to cry for him." Coker claims that he had hoped to call upon Mrs. Thomas during the sentencing phase, but that she disappeared after being told that she would have to remain outside in the hallway because witnesses are prohibited from hearing the testimony of other witnesses. Even though she was present at the courthouse on the day of the sentencing hearing, Coker failed to call her as a witness. As Bright and Canan pointed out on appeal, Coker made no other efforts to secure evidence in mitigation. They noted:

> **Had he done so, he would have unearthed a wealth of mitigating evidence which would have fundamentally changed the character and tone of the sentencing hearing. Instead, when the jury exited the courtroom to begin its deliberations on whether Mr. Thomas should live or die, it had not heard any mitigating evidence, and it knew very little about Mr. Thomas' character and station in life.**

. . . .

The first thing Canan, Kendall, and Bright did upon receiving Donny's record was file for an extension of sixty days. Shortly before they filed the cert. petition with the U.S. Supreme Court, the court overturned another Georgia case, *Godfrey v. Georgia*, based on its conclusion that the aggravating circumstance of "outrageously vile, horrible and inhuman" in the Georgia death penalty statute was unconstitutionally vague. The U.S. Supreme Court then vacated (voided) the decision of the Supreme Court of Georgia in Donny's case insofar as it affirmed the death penalty and remanded the case for further consideration in light of *Godfrey.*

Bright, Kendall, and Canan immediately filed a motion with the Georgia Supreme Court requesting an opportunity to file a brief and conduct an oral argument on the case, since several significant issues had not been raised in the eleven-page brief filed earlier on appeal. Their efforts were in vain. The Georgia Supreme Court sent back its opinion by return mail. In a mere one and a half pages, the court distinguished the facts of *Godfrey* and reaffirmed Donny's conviction. Bright, Kendall, and Canan again petitioned the U.S. Supreme Court for certiorari, arguing that the Georgia Supreme Court had neither taken Donny's case seriously nor properly applied *Godfrey*. Their second petition for certiorari was denied on September 23, 1981.

Bright remembers feeling shocked and discouraged at the Supreme Court's handling of Donny's case, even though he wasn't naive enough to expect the Court to grant certiorari. The speedy and superficial resolution of the case so far shook his belief that a winning issue was all that was needed to prevent Donny's execution. Aside from the legal issues in the case, Bright was not at all convinced that Donny was guilty. In his mind, there were two plausible possibilities: Cook and Lowe could have been pressured into saying that Donny had admitted the crime to them, or Donny could have falsely claimed that he killed Baugus in order to impress Cook. But proving Donny's innocence would have little worth if he did not first save his life.

. . . .

Shortly after the three lawyers agreed to take the case, Canan flew to Atlanta to meet with Donny. Patsy Morris accompanied Canan to the Fulton County Jail, where he introduced himself to Donny and explained that he, Kendall, and Bright had taken over his case. It was immediately apparent to him that Donny was mentally ill.

"This kid is really out of it," Canan told Bright and Kendall upon his return. "We're not going to be able to get anything out of him."

Donny struck Canan as even younger than his nineteen years because of his small frame and catatonic state. He seemed to be heavily sedated and depressed.

"This is pathetic," Canan thought to himself. "This is a guy in grave mental health distress who is disintegrating in front of me." He did not even seem to comprehend who Canan was or that he had a new set of attorneys. It was not until Canan was able to talk to Donny's relatives and former employers and teachers that a different portrait of his client began to emerge. Canan did not need to elicit a lot of information from Donny initially, however, since he was bound by the record for purposes of the cert. petition.

. . . .

After losing their cert. petition to the U.S. Supreme Court in 1981, Bright, Canan, and Kendall initiated state habeas proceedings by filing a petition for habeas corpus relief in the Superior Court of Butts County, Georgia. The petition raised a number of claims, including the assertion that Coker had provided ineffective assistance of counsel at Donny's trial. In Georgia, state habeas petitions are filed in the county where the condemned inmate is confined, rather than where he was originally tried. Judge J. Alex Crumley, the Butts County Supreme Court judge who received their petition, was coincidentally a former law partner of Judge Charles Waltner, who had presided over Donny's trial. Judge Crumley promptly granted their request for an evidentiary hearing, and scheduled it for February 11, 1982.

All three lawyers made several trips to Atlanta to investigate the issue and support their claim. By doing what Coker should have done in the first place, they hoped to be able to prove that there might very well have been a different outcome if Coker had defended Donny effectively. This was most apparent and easiest to prove at the sentencing phase, where it was clear that Coker did little to discover who Donny was as a person. As they stated in their brief, even minimal efforts on Coker's part "would have unearthed a wealth of mitigating evidence which would have fundamentally changed the character and tone of the sentencing hearing."

All three men acknowledge that the door to Donny's life story was opened by Elaine Gordon, an Antioch law student who was assisting them with legal research on the case. While she was home in Georgia with her family during her Christmas break in 1981, Gordon investigated Donny's work, family, and school history. In the short time she was home, she managed to track down and document a tremendous amount of mitigating evidence, all of which could have been presented at Donny's original sentencing.

In over one hundred pages of testimony at the state habeas hearing, former employers, teachers, counselors, coaches, family, and friends described Donny's life up to the time of his arrest. Frances Long, the manager who supervised Donny at Grandma's Biscuits, described him as the best employee she had ever supervised. Clyde Sweeney, another of Donny's former employers, agreed with Long's portrayal of Donny as a conscientious and trusted employee, noting that if he were ever to have another son, he would want him to be like Donny. Sammy Wells, the coach of the Roosevelt High School football team, remembered Donny as someone who was too small to play on the team but nonetheless came to practice every day and tried to participate in whatever way he could. Eugene Jones, a high school counselor, recalled Donny coming to him for counseling because of his unstable home environment. Both Sweeney and Wells noted that Donny's determination and commitment to overcome his shortcomings earned him the "most improved" student award one year.

More than fourteen witnesses testified on Donny's behalf at the state habeas hearing. Aside from what the witnesses had to say, the mere fact that Donny's attorneys were able to locate these witnesses from as far as 600 miles away reinforced the point that Coker could easily have done more on Donny's behalf. Had he simply picked up the phone, he could have lined up an impressive array of witnesses who would have been more than willing to testify and "contribute to a verbal mural of [Donny], portraying him as a good son, a respectful and hardworking young man, a non-violent, peaceful, and honest neighbor."

In addition to arguing that Coker failed to investigate and present evidence in mitigation at the penalty phase of the trial, Bright, Canan, and Kendall also focused on Coker's failure to properly investigate and demonstrate Donny's incompetence to stand trial. Coker acknowledged, when he took the stand during the state habeas evidentiary hearing, that Donny "would sit in his part of the visiting room and rock back and forth and would not communicate with me." He also testified that Donny sat throughout the trial with his right arm raised and his fist "in a clenched appearance," and that he was unable to persuade Donny "to refrain from this inappropriate behavior."

Bright and Canan were confident they had prevailed with at least some of their claims. The hearing had gone well in terms of what they were able to present to the court, and it seemed to them that the state did little to further its position and counter the evidence presented on Donny's behalf. They were also encouraged by Judge Crumley's questions and demeanor, which led them to believe that he thought the issues they had presented were sound.

Bright and Canan returned to Washington, D.C., full of optimism. They applauded Gordon for her contributions to what they were sure would be a victory. They assured Kendall that the hearing could not have gone any better. They also spent many late nights working on their brief, which Judge Crumley had given them thirty days to file. On March 8, 1982, less than one month after the hearing and before they even had a chance to submit their brief, Judge Cromwell issued an order denying habeas corpus relief on all grounds. Bright, Canan, and Kendall were devastated. They filed an application in the Supreme Court of Georgia asking it to review Judge Crumley's decision, but they were not the least bit surprised when the application was denied on June 2, 1982. Their third cert. petition to the U.S. Supreme Court was also denied on November 1, 1982.

Now that all of the state habeas appeals had been exhausted, the state set May 15, 1984, as the date for Donny's execution. His attorneys were able to obtain a stay on May 11, 1984. Once again, they had bought Donny some time. They hoped, however, that the federal courts would allow them to do more than that.

. . . .

In September 1992, Bright left Washington, D.C., and moved to Atlanta to become director of the Southern Prisoners' Defense Commission. Now renamed the Southern Center for Human Rights, it is a small, nonprofit organization that represents Death Row inmates and challenges unconstitutional prison and jail conditions throughout the South. Canan followed him to Atlanta in January 1993, and Kendall moved to Atlanta in April 1993 to do death penalty work for the ACLU.

Bright's investigative efforts on Donny's behalf intensified once he was able to devote more time to the case in Atlanta. He developed and pursued several alternative theories for the crime, all in an effort to clear Donny outright and all to no avail. Bright's first approach was to try to connect Dewey Baugus's murder with the infamous child murders that terrorized Atlanta in the early 1980s. By 1982, Wayne Williams was convicted of killing two black boys, but he was blamed for the deaths of two dozen black children. When Baugus was murdered, the police had not yet connected any of the murders or considered the possibility of a serial killer. Baugus's murder was distinctive because he was a white victim and all of the others were black. But Bright thought Baugus could still have been one of Williams's victims because Baugus lived in a virtually all-black neighborhood.

Bright met with the police task force dedicated to solving the serial murders, and he also spoke with the Fulton County police chief.

"I don't think Donny did it," the chief agreed when Bright confronted him with the evidence. "But that's just my opinion."

Bright approached the district attorney who had tried Donny in the hope that she would reconsider his case in light of the subsequent developments in Wayne Williams's case, but she was adamant in her refusal to do so. As far as she was concerned, the conviction she had originally obtained was proper and just; it was clear she would not back down.

Like Donny, Wayne Williams has continued to maintain his innocence. Unlike Donny, however, Williams was sentenced to two consecutive life terms for killing the two boys. Even though Williams was convicted of two murders rather than Donny's single murder conviction, and despite the fact that the police closed two dozen other cases after Williams's convictions because they assumed he was the perpetrator, the state never pursued the death penalty against Williams.

Bright's investigative efforts also unearthed the fact that there were other possible suspects for Baugus's murder. In particular, Bright discovered that nine-year-old Dewey Baugus had been involved in child pornography. Even though Bright was unable to prove that the victim's involvement in child pornography played a role in his murder, it was certainly the kind of evidence that could lead a jury to consider the possibility that someone else may have killed him. At trial the state has the burden of proving a defendant's guilt. After the trial, however, the burden is on the defendant to prove his innocence. Coker need only have alerted the jury to the possibility of other explanations for Baugus's murder to raise a reasonable doubt as to Donny's guilt, while Bright and his colleagues now had to actually prove Donny's innocence.

. . . .

By the time Bright and Kendall filed the federal habeas corpus petition, Canan had returned to Washington, D.C. Even prior to his departure, Bright and Kendall had taken over primary responsibility for the case because there were so many others requiring Canan's time and attention. Although Donny appreciated the fact that Bright, Kendall, and Canan had taken over his case on a pro bono basis, he did not realize what an embarrassment of riches he had enjoyed. Many defendants are never able to find counsel, let alone good counsel. Donny had had three dedicated attorneys, all of them defending capital cases on a full-time basis, jointly working on his case. His recollection many years later, however, was that he provided "three guys who were fresh out of school with the opportunity to prove to themselves that they were lawyers."

In addition to filing their petition with the U.S. District Court for the Northern District of Georgia, Bright and Kendall requested an evidentiary hearing. Even though they had developed a strong record in the state court proceedings, they convinced Judge Richard Freeman, who was presiding over their case, that it was crucial that he hear the witnesses in person. Judge Freeman agreed to a limited hearing, which took place on February 28 and March 1, 1985. Bright and Kendall presented two psychiatrists and some of the witnesses who had testified at the state habeas hearing.

The attorneys for the state of Georgia called a psychiatrist from Central State Hospital to reiterate his assessment that Donny was mentally competent. They also called Coker, who had left the public defender's office to become a prosecutor.

Coker's testimony about Donny's demeanor during trial was significantly more subdued than his earlier testimony during the state habeas hearing. He indicated that Donny's arm was only slightly raised and hovered just above the table, and that it was so subtle that he doubted anyone had even noticed. Bright aggressively confronted Coker with his previous testimony in the state court.

"Mr. Bright," Judge Freeman chastised him. "Mr. Coker is *not* on trial here."

In addition to arguing that the state trial court should have conducted an evidentiary hearing on Donny's competence to stand trial, Bright and Kendall asserted that the court gave the jury a constitutionally insufficient jury charge as to mitigating circumstances at sentencing and that the court had improperly dismissed members of the jury pool who were opposed to the death penalty. They also asserted that Coker had provided Donny with ineffective assistance of counsel at his sentencing by failing to present mitigating evidence.

On July 19, 1985, the U.S. District Court set aside the death sentence but upheld Donny's conviction. The court agreed that Donny's sentence was unconstitutional on two grounds: Coker's failure to present mitigating evidence at the sentencing and the trial court's insufficient jury charge as to mitigating circumstances. The court denied, however, all of Donny's other claims.

Bright and Kendall were surprised and dismayed by their loss on the competency issue, since they again felt that they had presented a strong case during the evidentiary hearing. They were relieved, however, to have prevailed on the sentencing issue. Even though the conviction remained intact, Donny was at least out from under the imminent threat of death.

The district court's decision with regard to the sentencing essentially remanded the case to the trial court for a new sentencing hearing. But in practice, the expenditure of time and resources could be (and often is) easily circumvented by having both sides agree on a new sentence of life imprisonment. The court would then sanction the agreement to simply change the sentence to life. A new sentencing hearing would have to be held, however, if the state intended to pursue the death penalty again.

Bright approached Joe Drolet at the district attorney's office. "Let's not appeal this," he proposed. "Just give him life and we'll leave it at that."

Drolet laughed and refused, informing Bright that the state absolutely planned to appeal. Bright and Kendall then cross-appealed on the competency issue.

When the case came before three judges of the U.S. Court of Appeals for the Eleventh Circuit, one judge asked Assistant Attorney General Mary Beth Westmoreland, "Is it the policy of your office to just appeal no matter what?"

"That sounds promising," Bright whispered to Kendall.

On July 28, 1986, the court of appeals affirmed the district court's ruling with respect to the ineffective assistance of counsel at Donny's sentencing, but denied relief on all the other grounds.

. . . .

Bright and Kendall were relieved that Donny's death sentence had again been deemed unconstitutional, but were disappointed that the court of appeals had left his conviction intact. They therefore filed a final cert. petition with the U.S. Supreme Court, adding to their previous claims the assertion that Donny's Sixth Amendment right to the assistance of counsel was violated when he was refused counsel at his preliminary hearing. On

December 1, 1986, the U.S. Supreme Court once again denied certiorari, ruling that the denial of counsel at the preliminary hearing was a harmless error.

With his appeals exhausted, Donny had no choice but to await the next move from the state regarding his sentencing. His case had been remanded to Judge Osgood Williams, rather than to the judge who had presided over the original trial. Generally, the protocol in such situations is for the court to schedule a new sentencing hearing, unless the state agrees to a sentence of life. At the time, convictions for murder in Georgia allowed for only two possibilities: a life sentence, with the possibility of parole, or a sentence of death. Today there is the additional sentencing option of life without the possibility of parole.

While he was waiting for the state to approach him about Donny's case, Bright received a letter from the clerk of the Superior Court of Fulton County. Upon opening it, he was surprised to find an order sentencing Donald Wayne Thomas to life imprisonment. Bright had not contacted the court or the state, nor had they solicited any input from him.

After sharing the good news with Kendall and with Canan, who had continued to follow Donny's progress after leaving Atlanta, Bright went to see Donny at Georgia State Prison in Reidsville, Georgia.

"It's over," Bright told Donny, but it was clear Donny had trouble comprehending any end other than his execution.

"No more appeals?" Donny asked.

"No, that's it," Bright assured him. "This is your sentence."

"I didn't do it," Donny said again, as he did each time Bright visited him.

. . . .

The time Donny spent on Death Row took a terrible toll on him. He is a small man, and he lived in constant fear of being raped by another Death Row inmate. He also continued to suffer psychotic episodes, but worried about his ability to defend himself when he took his medications.

"If I take the medicine, I get woozy and then I can't protect myself," he once complained to Bright. "But if I don't, I go nuts."

He is relieved to be off Death Row, but he continues to covet his freedom.

"Prison life," he says, "is living hell." Donny describes an environment in which everyone fears for his own life, and confusion and hate abound.

He maintains that he does not suffer from any type of mental illness, but that not being able to urinate (from an apparent bladder infection, for which he also takes medication) makes him "crazy in the head."

Even though Donny was eligible for parole in 1986, after having served seven years in prison, he remains incarcerated. The same mental problems that were deemed insufficient to qualify him as mentally incompetent to stand trial now prevent him from reentering society.

When he got a phone call last year telling him his mother died, he said, "It was like an atomic bomb going off inside." His only comfort is his religious fervor, which stems from the time he had a vision of God while on Death Row.

"He told me to feed my sheep," Donny explains. It was at that point that Donny stopped fretting about his case, and instead promised God that he would do what He wanted. Another inmate, Warren McClesky, who was later executed, introduced Donny to the Bible and worked with him to improve his reading and writing abilities. Donny has since written to President Clinton, sending him hundreds of pages of Bible prophesies that God revealed to him.

"The president needs them in order to achieve for this country," Donny says. "God sent me to him. It's my job."

michael cervi

Michael Cervi enlisted in the U.S. Navy in the fall of 1975, having graduated from Tennyson High School in Hayward, California, the previous spring. After boot camp in San Diego, Michael attended Gunner's Mate School at the Naval Training Center in Great Lake, New York, where he received vocational training in electricity. By 1977, he had been transferred to the U.S.S. *Santa Barbara*, a munitions ship stationed in Charleston, South Carolina. It was a tough time to be in the service. The Vietnam War was still fresh in the public's memory, and there was no longer much prestige associated with being in the military. Enlisted men were especially disrespected, and morale among them was low.

Many of the men on Michael's ship passed the time by smoking marijuana and drinking heavily. Michael did so as well, but he was able to avoid detection and received good reviews for his work. Unlike his buddy Robby Wilson, who joined the crew directly from boot camp and was therefore assigned menial jobs, Michael was made a gunner's mate and was even given security clearance. He nonetheless put in for a transfer because he longed to be on a ship that had guns rather than just ammunition so he could truly be a gunner's mate. It was only when Michael's request for a transfer was denied that he began to strategize about other means of getting off the ship.

Wilson wished to leave the navy altogether, and he convinced Michael to hitchhike to Nebraska with him. From there, Michael planned to fly back to California, where he would reenlist on a ship more to his liking. He figured his "unauthorized leave" would not count as desertion as long as he was not absent from the service for more than thirty days. On Saturday, February 23, 1977, both men simply walked off the ship. They spent the night at a friend's trailer nearby, where they gathered their belongings, including the 30–30 Marlin rifle Michael had stored there.

The first ride they received took them to Columbia, South Carolina, where they were picked up by Dr. Kenneth Lawrence, who was on his way to Atlanta. Wilson sat up front with the doctor while Michael stretched out in the backseat. When Dr. Lawrence stopped and went inside a fast food restaurant for dinner, the two hitchhikers spontaneously decided to rob him of his money and steal his car. This was not something Michael had ever done before, or even contemplated. In his only prior brush with the law, he was arrested for possession of marijuana.

Just outside Augusta, Georgia, Michael took his rifle out of his sea bag and ordered Dr. Lawrence to exit off the interstate onto U.S. 278. After taking Dr. Lawrence's money, Michael and Wilson marched him about 150 yards off the road into a wooded area, where they tied him to a tree using his necktie. Michael transferred the rifle to Wilson at this point, who proceeded to hit Dr. Lawrence in the head several times with the butt of it. Michael then stabbed the doctor three times in the neck, maintaining later that Wilson had pointed the rifle at him and ordered him to do so. The two took off in Dr. Lawrence's car; Michael was driving.

Michael had been in fights before, but never anything that generated this much blood. The sight of the blood scared him; he was pretty sure the doctor would die. His adrenaline was rushing, and he couldn't think clearly. The only thought he could grasp, which repeated itself in his mind like a mantra, was "We gotta get outta here!"

Dr. Lawrence managed to free himself and get to the highway, where he was picked up and taken to a local hospital. He died the next day, but not before identifying Wilson and Michael as his assailants.

On the morning of March 3, 1977, an Iowa state trooper, James Brumbaugh, stopped a car for speeding in Mills County, Iowa. Michael was in such a daze that it wasn't until he heard the sirens behind him that he realized they were still driving the doctor's car. "Oh shit," he thought. "We're done."

A check on their driver's licenses revealed that Michael and Wilson were wanted for murder in Georgia.

"We got you," the trooper said. There was no point in denying it.

. . . .

Even though she had just finished eating breakfast, Juanita Cervi was busy making dinner. She no longer had to make quite as much, because her older son, Michael, was in the Navy, but she still liked to have dinner ready each night for her younger son, Ron, and her husband, Bernie. In the midst of her preparations, Bernie surprised her by walking in the door, accompanied by several other men. Bernie was the chief homicide detective for Alameda County, California, and Juanita knew he was supposed to be testifying in a homicide case all morning. Had the men shown up without Bernie, Juanita would have been terrified. Every sheriff's wife lives in fear of her husband's colleagues showing up at the house with somber expressions. It was, after all, a dangerous profession. But here was Bernie alive and well, so Juanita couldn't imagine what could possibly be wrong.

Bernie sat down on the sofa. He could not even bring himself to look at Juanita, but instead turned his head away.

"Michael's in a lot of trouble," one of the men said.

"It's not Michael. It can't be," Bernie blurted out. "Someone must have stolen his ID."

Juanita had just begun processing the fact that it was Michael who had prompted Bernie to come home in the middle of the morning, when one of the men said, "Michael's killed someone."

Bernie turned to look at her then, to see her reaction. Juanita was only dimly aware of him, because she was too stunned to register anything but the awful news that her son had committed murder. She simply couldn't believe it; it was completely out of character. To be sure, Michael had been a difficult teenager, but no more so than other children who grew up in the sixties. With his long hair and pot-smoking, he was often at odds with his father. But he was a good kid, the kind who would literally give you the shirt off his back. It just couldn't be true.

Bernie asked one of the men to please call the navy. "I'm sure he's still on the base," he said. "And then we can straighten this whole thing out."

While his colleague did as he was asked, Bernie filled Juanita in on the details of the crime. Juanita stared at him incredulously, feeling that her whole world had just irrevocably changed. Later in the day, Cindy Yip arrived at the house, having been called at her job at J.C. Penny. Cindy was Michael's high school sweetheart; the two had just started looking at rings and planning an engagement. Even though she was in the most frequent contact with Michael, it was soon apparent that Cindy knew nothing about what had happened.

When Ron got home from school, one of the men gave him the devastating news. Juanita wanted to be the one to tell him, but she simply couldn't. For the next three days, she could not talk, eat, or sleep.

Bernie was also devastated, but he had to return to court. The trial that had been interrupted with the news about Michael couldn't be delayed any longer. At least he was surrounded by attorneys, so that he was able to get some names of good criminal lawyers in Iowa, where Michael had been apprehended, and in Georgia, where he was going to be tried.

Juanita and Bernie hastily arranged to fly to Iowa.

"Whatever happens," Juanita reassured her husband, "we still have each other."

. . . .

The trooper who pulled Michael and Wilson over for speeding arrested them and transported them to the Mills County Jail in Glenwood, Iowa. That afternoon, they were both brought before Magistrate Esther Engle for an extradition hearing. Magistrate Engle asked Michael if he wanted counsel, and he answered yes, so she adjourned the proceedings until counsel could be obtained.

Walter Green, the Iowa prosecutor, called James Thomas, a local attorney, and asked him if he would take both cases. Thomas agreed to represent both men, but stated that he would not be able to do so until the following morning. Magistrate Engle then appointed Mr. Thomas as counsel for both defendants and delayed the hearing until 10:00 the following morning, March 4.

At some point before 9:30 on that morning, the Georgia district attorney Kenneth Goolsby and the Georgia Bureau of Investigation (GBI) agent Robert Ingram arrived at the Mills County sheriff's office. At their request, Michael was brought to the sheriff's office from the jail and taken to a private room. Ingram read Michael a standard *Miranda* form (indicating that he had the right to an attorney and that, if he were to waive that right, everything he said could be used against him in a court of law), which Michael signed. Ingram then summarized the evidence against him, and Michael confessed orally to the crime. After obtaining Michael's permission to do so, Ingram wrote out Michael's confession, which Michael signed at 10:56 A.M.

Meanwhile, James Thomas, who had been appointed the previous day to represent Michael, arrived at the courthouse. Starting at 9:15 A.M., he made two requests to see his clients, both of which were denied. At 9:30, Thomas stepped into a nearby office, where Green and Goolsby were conferring, and insisted that he be allowed to see his clients. The prosecutors refused his request. He made one final demand at 9:45 A.M., which was also denied. Michael was never advised of Thomas's presence.

Later that morning, at the extradition hearing, Thomas made sure he put the events surrounding the confession on record, including his repeated and unsuccessful requests for access to his clients. Michael then waived extradition, which meant that he agreed not to fight Georgia in its right to try him there rather than in Iowa, and Goolsby and Ingram took him back to Georgia.

. . . .

Bernie, Juanita, and Cindy flew to Iowa, only to find that Michael had already been extradited to Georgia. They promptly flew to Atlanta after briefly meeting with an Iowa attorney named Matt Walsh, whom they had contacted prior to leaving California. Walsh had already spoken with Thomas and knew the details of the confession. He told the Cervis enough to convince them that Michael had been involved in the murder. Cindy, however, continued to believe it was all a mistake that would soon be cleared up.

The trip seemed interminable to Juanita, who was desperate to see her son. Even though she could no longer deny his wrongdoing, he was still her beloved son. She knew a mother's love could withstand even murder, but she was unsure how Bernie would react to Michael. Her fears were allayed when they met with Toby Ivey, the local attorney who had been recommended to them in California.

Ivey, a tall, charismatic Georgia native, had a successful general practice in Augusta, Georgia, that included four previous death penalty cases. He had obtained not guilty verdicts in all four cases, although one had to be retried three times. Ivey agreed to take Michael's case, but informed them that he would need a $5,000 retainer fee. Juanita remembers looking at her husband apprehensively, not yet knowing the extent of his support for their son.

"We'll get you the money, and whatever else it takes," Bernie said, "even if we have to sell our house." Juanita knew then that Bernie, the homicide detective, was first and foremost the father of their son.

They met with Michael separately, since only one of them was allowed to see him at a time. Michael was incarcerated in McDuffie County, rather than in Taliaferro County, where the crime had occurred, because of the absence of a jail facility in that county. Juanita reassured Michael that she loved him and that both she and Bernie were there for him, no matter what. Michael had just turned nineteen, but he looked like a scared, little boy to Juanita. She was overwhelmed with the need to take him into her arms and take him home. But she couldn't do that. Not now, and possibly not ever.

．．．．．．．．

When Michael met Toby Ivey for the first time, he could tell Ivey was furious.

"What the hell is this?" Ivey asked Michael, throwing down that day's *Atlanta Constitution*. The paper had a photo of Michael stepping off the plane, grinning. "What in God's graces were you so happy about, son?" Ivey asked him. "Doesn't seem to me like you've got a whole lot to smile about." Michael said something about the photographer intentionally tripping to elicit a smile from him, but Ivey wasn't done with his tirade.

"And this," he said with disgust, throwing down a copy of Michael's seventeen-page confession. "What on earth possessed you to bare your soul? That Wilson boy, all he said was, 'He's dead. I'm sorry.' But you wrote a goddamn novel."

By the time Ivey left, however, Michael had total confidence in the attorney his parents had retained for him. He knew he had really screwed up and that he was going to have to serve some time, but he was equally sure Ivey would keep him from getting a death sentence.

．．．．．．．．

Ivey was realistic with the Cervis about Michael's prospects. He did not expect to prevail at Michael's trial, since Michael's detailed confession rendered a not guilty verdict almost impossible, despite the fact that the confession was unconstitutionally obtained. The most he could accomplish, and what he was ultimately striving for, was to avoid the death penalty. He also hoped to establish a good record for the appeals process.

With the appellate record in mind, Ivey put Michael on the stand during a hearing on his motion to suppress Michael's confession in order to establish some of the details surrounding the confession. He had hoped to limit Michael's testimony, but the judge ruled that the prosecutor, Kenneth Goolsby—the same prosecutor who was present in Iowa during the contested confession—was entitled to cross-examine Michael. When Goolsby asked Michael about the details of the confession itself, Ivey directed Michael to invoke the Fifth Amendment and not answer on the ground that it might incriminate him. This tactic served only to infuriate Goolsby, and he later took out his frustrations on Michael during the sentencing phase. As Ivey reported to the Cervis in a letter describing the trial, the "real clincher resulted from another portion of Mike's testimony, and what transpired is both unfortunate and understandable."

Michael had always maintained that when GBI agent Ingram first confronted him in Iowa, Michael asked about an attorney and Ingram pointed at Goolsby across the room and responded, "He's an attorney." Michael therefore concluded that since this was his attorney, he was free to talk fully, and, if he said anything contrary to his best interest, the attorney would stop him. On the stand, however, Michael went even further and stated that Goolsby, rather than passively sitting by during Ingram's deception, affirmatively stated, "Yes, I am," and aggressively shook his head in agreement.

In his letter to the Cervis, Ivey spelled out the repercussions of Michael's incriminating testimony about Goolsby:

> **At this juncture, the District Attorney was barely coherent, and told the court that he was going to take the witness stand at trial and then proceeded to repeat a series of callous, and incriminating remarks he allegedly overheard Mike make during the trip back to Georgia. It is not surprising that these were uncorroborated.**
>
> **In order to place this travesty in any sort of perspective, you must realize and understand that the main actors are a District Attorney and a Superior Court Judge, who are the only District Attorney and Judge in a rural Georgia circuit, and who have been trying cases in this fashion for twenty years. While I do not disbelieve Mike, I regretted—as does he—the fact that his testimony went beyond what was necessary and needlessly offended the shark in his home waters.**

The jury selection also proved to be an omen of the case's eventual outcome; it did not go Michael's way either. Ivey first moved for a change of venue, arguing that the jurors in Taliaferro County would be prejudiced against Michael. Not only had there been a great deal of prejudicial publicity, but Taliaferro County juries had tried capital cases in the last three consecutive terms of court, all of which involved nonresident victims and nonresident defendants; and all the defendants were convicted and sentenced to death. Ivey also feared that Taliaferro County residents would resent the fact that Michael's trial would eat up a quarter of the county's annual tax revenues, causing either taxes to be increased or services diminished. The judge, heeding the jurors' contentions that these factors would not influence them in any way, declined to assign the case to another circuit.

The judge also declined Ivey's subsequent request for a change of venue once the jury was impaneled, disagreeing with Ivey's assertion that it did not represent a legitimate cross-section of the county. At that time, Taliaferro County had a population of 2,300 people; 70 percent were black and 30 percent, white. During the process of qualifying the jury, eighty-nine black jurors were disqualified because they would not impose capital punishment under any circumstances. Another nine were struck. The result was an all-white jury in a county whose population was less than one-third white. Although Michael was white, his jury nevertheless should have been more representative of the county in which he was being tried.

Ivey did not fare much better with his motions and requests during the trial. From various medical personnel who treated Dr. Lawrence after his injuries, Ivey was able to elicit that the doctor's death certificate showed the cause of death as "aspiration pneumonia." However, he was severely limited in what he was allowed to ask the doctor who represented the hospital where Dr. Lawrence had died. Ivey was nonetheless able to get the doctor to acknowledge that Dr. Lawrence could have died of the same condition without receiving any injuries. This seemed a huge victory at the time; it seemed to entitle Michael to a charge on intervening cause, as well as on the lesser included offense of involuntary manslaughter, but the judge refused to include either in his instructions to the jury.

On February 29, 1980, Michael Cervi was convicted of murder, kidnapping, armed robbery, and motor vehicle theft in the Superior Court of Taliaferro County. After five days of trial, the jury took only an hour and fifteen minutes to reach a verdict of guilty. The sentencing hearing immediately followed the conviction. Ivey put Michael on the stand again (having done so during the suppression hearing but not during the trial), and Goolsby proceeded to ask him several questions that prompted Ivey to make several requests for a mistrial. Goolsby first asked Michael, "Mr. Cervi, you claim to be a Christian, but isn't it true that you tried to withhold evidence from this court by taking the Fifth Amendment?" Ivey objected strenuously, and Judge Stevens instructed the jury to disregard Goolsby's question. Goolsby next asked Michael, "Mr. Cervi, you claim to be a Christian, but isn't it true that you withheld evidence from this court by pleading not guilty?" Ivey again objected vehemently, and more precautionary instructions were given to the jury. But Ivey knew at that point that a death sentence was inevitable. He wrote to the Cervis, "From that point on, I knew without any doubt what the outcome would be. I also knew that it really didn't matter since no appellate court would possibly tolerate such conduct."

. . . .

On January 27, 1980, Bernie Cervi was diagnosed with testicular cancer. By the time he was tested, the cancer had already progressed to his lymph nodes, and he was given less than six months to live. His chemotherapy began immediately, making it impossible for him to attend Michael's trial the following month. Instead, he arranged for a family friend to accompany Juanita to Georgia.

Juanita tried to be positive when she called home to Bernie each night to let him know the day's developments, but she was never as hopeful as she sounded. Michael's trial didn't correspond at all to what she had envisioned. In the movies, courtroom proceedings usually appear to be balanced and fair, but Michael's trial seemed horribly skewed against him. Juanita noticed right away that the prosecutor and the judge seemed to be good friends, and that the prosecutor seemed to know or be on friendly terms with all of the potential jurors. "Oh, you're Charlie Smith," he would say. "Why, your daddy and I used to go fishing together when we were boys." Ivey, by contrast, knew no one and struck Juanita as a lone outsider.

Then there were the jurors themselves. One potential juror, when asked about his views on the death penalty, responded, "Well, I think there are too many people in jail and we should just start killing them." Even though he wasn't selected, Juanita knew he represented what they were up against. She began to fear not just a guilty verdict, but the looming possibility of a death sentence as well.

In addition to the friend who had accompanied her from California, Juanita was comforted by the Ponders, a Georgia couple who had befriended Michael and traveled over one hundred miles to visit him every week. Aside from them, however, Juanita definitely did not feel welcome in Taliaferro County. One day during the trial, she and the Ponders went to a local restaurant to eat lunch. While everyone around them ordered and was served their meals, "the murderer's table" received nothing but angry stares. Juanita returned to the courtroom with an empty stomach and a heavy heart, convinced that the experience was a sign of things to come.

On February 29, 1980, Juanita's worst fears were realized. Having been found guilty on all counts the day before, Michael was sentenced to death. The hardest part for Juanita came that night, when she had to call Bernie back home and tell him that their son was going to be sent to the chair.

. . . .

Robby Wilson was tried next, but his trial differed from Michael's in several significant respects. In contrast to the five days of testimony and numerous live witnesses in Michael's trial, Robby's consisted almost exclusively of stipulations and lasted only three hours. Wilson, who had observed Michael's trial each day along with his attorney, seemed to have learned from Michael's mistakes. The district attorney, as Ivey later described it to the Cervis, "had vented his spleen, and had no personal vendetta against Robby." The jury was also dealing with a much less lengthy and detailed confession in Wilson's case, three pages as compared with Michael's seventeen pages. Perhaps the most important difference in the two trials, however, was something that could not have been predicted. When Wilson's jury began their deliberations about his punishment, an emergency weather alert was flashed throughout Georgia, emphasizing that roads would become impassable that evening and that virtually no vehicular movement would be possible. Judge Stevens alerted the jury and permitted them fifteen minutes in which to make a decision: They could either immediately agree on Wilson's sentence or face an indeterminate period of confinement while they deliberated. They chose to sentence Wilson to life imprisonment.

. . . .

Cindy always believed Michael was innocent. There was no way the man she loved, whom she'd known since he was in the ninth grade, could have killed anyone. In fact, one of the things that attracted her to Michael was his compassion for others. He was not a violent person. Unlike Michael's parents, who had spoken with Ivey and knew the extent of

Michael's involvement with Dr. Lawrence's death, Cindy had never discussed the particulars of the crime with Michael or anyone else.

As devastated as she was about Michael's death sentence, she nonetheless believed that justice would ultimately prevail and that he would be released. She wrote to Michael regularly and visited him several times in prison. In an effort to be closer to him, she applied to and was accepted by a college in Savannah, Georgia. Michael was not elated, however; he told her bluntly not to go. In a letter that broke Cindy's heart, Michael explained that he was severing all ties with her. "My life is over," he wrote, "and I refuse to drag you down with me." As Michael saw it, the best thing he could do for Cindy, the woman he loved, was to allow her to find happiness with someone else. It was one of the hardest things he had ever done. Cindy, who thought it was simply a matter of convincing Michael that she would stick with him, continued to write to him. It was only when Michael took her off his visitor's list that Cindy accepted the fact that he was out of her life for good.

. . . .

Michael's death sentence was not the only blow to the Cervi family. In May 1980, four months after he was first diagnosed with cancer, Bernie Cervi died. Michael took it hard, convinced that he had played a role in his father's illness and death. It had been difficult enough seeing his mother's anguish at his trial, but it had been even harder not having his father there. Bernie Cervi's death took on biblical proportions for Michael, who had rekindled his religious faith during his incarceration. The fact that his father died so soon after Michael was sentenced to death struck Michael as particularly prophetic. He repeatedly read King David's passage in 2 Samuel, in which he laments, "Oh Absalom, my son, my son. I would that I could have died in your place."

Another difficult adjustment for Michael was his transfer to Death Row at the Georgia Diagnostic and Classification Center in Jackson, Georgia. Even though his incarceration at McDuffie County jail had not been easy, it was nothing compared to Jackson. He was put on the H-2 cell block, referred to by the inmates as "Little Vietnam" because of the frequent stabbings that took place there. Michael soon learned that there were two powerful cliques: those inmates who had transferred from Reidsville Death

Row and those who were considered Jackson prisoners. Each clique had guards on its side, who could be bribed to set up fights and open cell doors so that the inmates could get at each other.

Michael certainly had it easier than many of his fellow inmates. He was blessed with a family that steadfastly stood by him, who wrote to him regularly, and sent him money for cigarettes. Michael not only appreciated his good fortune, but also shared it with others, often buying cigarettes for those inmates who had been completely abandoned by their families. Juanita remembers being touched by her son's concern over some of the others on Death Row, particularly those who struck him as obviously mentally ill. "They howl all night, Mom," he would tell her. "They don't belong here. They should be in a hospital or a mental institution."

Michael also had the help of older and more prison-savvy inmates who acted as his rescuers and mentors, protecting him and showing him the ropes. Billy Mitchell held off another inmate's attempt to make Michael his "punk," the prison's alternative to a girlfriend. Wes McCorquodale, known as "Big Wes," once picked Michael up and threw him back into his cell to prevent Michael from getting into a fight that Big Wes knew was a setup. Warren McClesky, known as "Pizon," taught Michael the code of never snitching to the officers. Andrew Lagare once intentionally got in trouble so that he could join Michael in "the hole," the prison's maximum security cells. All of the men who befriended Michael and helped him adjust to prison life became his close friends, and most were executed during Michael's time on Death Row.

. . . .

Ivey assured Juanita that he would immediately appeal Michael's conviction and sentence. The case was rich with appellate issues, he explained, and the trial had at least served to provide them with an excellent record with which to appeal. Juanita felt optimistic about Michael's chances, although the $5,000 Ivey needed to file each appeal was staggering. She nonetheless assured him that he should do whatever it took to free her son, and she would somehow get the money to him.

Even though Ivey raised several issues on appeal, the one he was absolutely convinced the Supreme Court of Georgia would see in Michael's favor involved Michael's confession and the fact that he had been denied an attorney after requesting one. As Ivey saw it, even a first-year law student would be able to recognize that Michael's constitutional rights had been violated.

Michael shared Ivey's confidence.

Mar. 15, 1981

Dear Mr. Ivey:

I am sorry for taking so long in getting back to you. I really read your, our, brief and then I had to reread it about three times to really understand it.

I think you did a magnificent job on it and I am sure we will get the death sentence overturned. As I see it, it looks as if you are trying to get a manslaughter charge out of this, can the supreme court give me this?

I especially like the beginning where you told them just the way it happened. Do you think it will take very long for them to decide? As I was looking deeper it seems to me that you have given us several areas in which we can go. If they strike the confession we can go to trial and maybe get time served? The change of vinue is also a good possibility as I think that another judge would let you cross examine Dr. Wills more thoroughly which is another thing I don't see how they can over look.

Mr. Ivey you can't imagine how grateful I am that you are working on my case there so many guys here who are depending on lawyers who really don't care and I am sure aren't as talented as you. You'll have to forgive me for going on like that, But I think you can understand my feelings.

Do you have any hunches as to on which ones the court will rule on in our favor? Hopefully everyone.

Any way I think you did an excellent job on the brief and I feel confident that I won't be here too much longer.

God Bless you,
Michael Cervi

Six months later, Michael's hope died. On September 29, 1981, the Supreme Court of Georgia affirmed his conviction and death sentence. He began to despair of ever getting out of prison. For the first time since he was arrested, he struggled to accept the notion that he would die there.

With respect to Michael's confession, the court ruled that "[t]he actions of the Georgia authorities were not a violation of the right to counsel as set forth by the U.S. Supreme Court in Edwards v. Arizona." The court disagreed with Ivey's contention that Michael's request for counsel at the Iowa probable-cause hearing precluded his interrogation by the Georgia investigators without notifying appointed counsel and allowing him to be present. Finding that Michael's request for counsel could be narrowly construed, the court ruled that "under the facts of this case, the appointment of counsel by one jurisdiction for the limited purpose of representation at a probable cause hearing and extradition proceeding, did not prevent the appellant from giving an informed waiver of counsel prior to interrogation by the requesting state."

October 23, 1981

> *Dear Mr. Ivey:*
>
> *Enclosed please find a money order for $2,000. I'm sorry it couldn't be more, but you can be sure that it isn't the last. I'd like to send you some more within the next few months.*
>
> *I'd like to say I know you are doing your best and that you are just as disappointed as we are with the decision of the Georgia Supreme Court. We would like you to know we still have complete confidence in you. I know you are doing all that can be done and I thank you for it. If there is anything we can do, please let us know. We feel so helpless, partly because we are so far away.*
>
> *We would like to know what our next step is and what we can expect to hear. I realize everything is such a waiting game but do you have any idea how much longer it will take to, at least, get the death sentence dropped? That is currently the most disturbing aspect of this situation.*
>
> *Thank you for your time.*
>
> *Sincerely,*
> *Juanita B. Cervi*

Ivey petitioned the U.S. Supreme Court for certiorari, but he was no longer as confident in his ability to prevail on the record. Once the Court denied certiorari, Ivey knew that the next step in the appellate process was to initiate state habeas proceedings. This was something he had never done before, having always prevailed at trial with his previous criminal clients.

. . . .

In December 1982, George Kendall returned to Washington, D.C., from a trip to Atlanta, where he was helping out at the Southern Prisoners' Defense Commission. Kendall soon got a call from Steve Bright: "Patsy Morris has raised $15,000 to hire an additional attorney for one year," Bright said. "How would you like to come down here?"

Kendall promised Bright he would think about it. His hesitation wasn't based on the substantial pay cut or the fact that he really enjoyed his job and his life in Washington, D.C. He had survived on similar salaries prior to law school, and he could always return to Washington. His primary concern in leaving was parting from his three-year-old nephew, who had recently suffered the loss of his father. What ultimately swayed Kendall was the realization that he would never again be as untethered and able to spontaneously pack up and go. Had he known then the extent to which the courts would allow executions to take place, he would have thought twice about devoting a year to capital defense work. At the time, though, he felt he could make a significant difference. So he packed up and joined Bright in Georgia.

When Kendall arrived in Atlanta in mid-April 1983, he was given responsibility for the Georgia caseload so that Bright and other attorneys at the Southern Prisoners' Defense Commission (SPDC) could focus their efforts on other southern states. The SPDC did not become involved with a case until after the first appeal failed. Usually, the trial attorney was already out of the picture by the time a case reached the SPDC, leaving the defendant with no counsel and often with little time to reverse the conviction or reduce the sentence. Kendall's role was to write the inevitable emergency pleadings that had to be filed to prevent an execution, and then to find another attorney to take over whenever possible.

The call from Toby Ivey came in mid-June 1983. Ivey informed Kendall that Michael had an execution date set for the following week and asked for his help. Kendall drove down to Augusta and met with Ivey. Even before meeting him, Kendall was impressed by Ivey's obvious commitment to Michael and by his determination to stick with the case. Many trial attorneys not only ducked out at the conclusion of the state appeal, they often turned hostile toward their clients. Ivey thought the case could be won, but he realized that he was not a death penalty attorney and he lacked the skills and experience to continue as lead counsel.

Kendall quickly prepared a habeas corpus petition, which Ivey then argued before Judge Hal Craig in the Butts County Superior Court. Even though Kendall and Ivey did not prevail, they were at least able to get a stay granted, and Michael's execution date was no longer imminent.

Kendall had been doing death penalty cases in Georgia for less than a year, but he had already amassed enough experience to view the state habeas process as a moot endeavor. In his mind, it was akin to driving through Baltimore and Philadelphia on the way to New York; you have to do it, but it serves no purpose. For the federal habeas petition, however, he decided to enlist the help of additional counsel.

In January 1985, Jim Doyle was the deputy director of the Criminal Justice Clinic at Georgetown University Law Center in Washington, D.C. He agreed to assist with Michael's case after Bright and Kendall "tag teamed" him. First Bright enticed him with the issue of a confession obtained under questionable circumstances, then Kendall followed, assuring him that he and Ivey would remain involved.

When Doyle first met Michael, he was struck by how much more solid and mature Michael was in person than he had appeared in the photos and case files he had reviewed. Michael impressed Doyle with how grateful he was for Ivey's efforts on his behalf. He made it clear to Doyle that he did not want him to go after Ivey, even if it would benefit his case. Doyle assured Michael that he would not be pursuing an ineffective assistance of counsel claim.

Despite Doyle's assurances to the contrary, Michael initially perceived Doyle as replacing Ivey, whom he had grown to trust and respect. After Doyle left, Michael instantly called his brother, Ron, in California and asked him to make sure Doyle did not succeed in kicking Ivey off his case. Ron Cervi immediately wrote to Ivey and conveyed Michael's concerns, telling him that Doyle's visit had really upset Michael. Ivey then called Kendall, essentially telling him, "If this is the kind of help you've lined up, forget it." Kendall promised to get to the bottom of it, and called up Doyle. A flurry of letters ensued.

February 6, 1985

Dear Mr. Ivey:

George Kendall relayed your concern over a letter you received from Mike Cervi's brother. It concerns me too.

It particularly concerns me because my primary goal in meeting Mike was to be sure *that he understood that—unlike virtually everyone else in his situation—he did* not *have an ineffective assistance of counsel claim. My fear was that he would assume that a change in lawyers would mean something of the kind.*

I am also concerned since, (as I hope Kendall told you), I have nothing but praise for the representation you provided under extraordinarily difficult circumstances. I cannot imagine, even with the benefit of hindsight, how I or anyone else could have done better.

Yours,
James Doyle

November 12, 1985

Dear Mr. Ivey:

We received your letter of Oct. 10th and can't help but feel good about it. I agree that any changes at all could only be positive. We thank you for your persistence and generosity.

We received our monthly phone call from Mike and he continues to be in good spirits. In one of his recent letters, he seemed somewhat concerned and apprehensive about your continuing in his defense and I assured him that you are still helping us. Your letter confirms this. I know that he feels a lot better knowing you are behind him, he has a very high regard for you and so do we.

Enclosed is a check for $1,000, again, I'm sorry for the delay. Again, thank you for all your help.

Juanita Cervi

Feb. 20

Dear Mr. Ivey:

I thought I should write you a few lines, due to the rumors, and speculation I've heard about you, and your involvement in my appeals.

I want to personally assure you that I have the utmost confidence in your abilities, and dedication.

I remember the last time I saw you; you told me of a conversation you had with my father. I will never forget it, and it reinforces my convictions in you.

In closing I would like to thank you for your excellent work on my be-

*half. We will be in the Augusta Federal Court soon, and I am sure that
everything will work out for us then.*

With respect and gratitude,
Michael Cervi

The misunderstanding was eventually cleared up, leaving Michael grateful that he now had three dedicated attorneys working on his behalf. He often marveled at his luck, having seen the dismal representation some of his fellow inmates had to contend with, not to mention those who had no attorney whatsoever. Ivey, Kendall, and Doyle certainly appreciated the unique role each of them played in Michael's case, and all three acknowledged the necessity of teamwork on Michael's behalf.

Ivey was the one who had been with Michael from the start; he was also the one who served as Michael's best shot at having an insider working for him—a local attorney who was part of the "good ol' boy" network. Kendall was the long-haired, bearded lawyer who instantly won Michael's trust by getting down to his level and cussing about the guards. And Doyle, initially so off-putting because of his suit and professorial demeanor, soon won Michael's respect and confidence with the incredible legal briefs he wrote on Michael's behalf.

Despite his attorneys' efforts, however, Michael did not feel a renewed sense of optimism about his prospects. He knew the violation of his right to counsel was a sound issue, but he had seen others executed whose cases were even more compelling than his own. He decided that when his time came, he would scale the prison fence in an attempt to be shot doing so. A quick, sure death from a bullet seemed preferable to the electric chair, particularly given the agony and emotional roller-coaster he had seen the families of his friends endure when their execution dates arrived. Only Kendall's visits managed to raise Michael's spirits significantly, but within a few weeks he would find himself once again resigned to his inevitable death.

. . . .

Neither Kendall nor Doyle held out great hope for how Michael's case would fare before the district court judge Dudley Bowen. This was, after all, a conservative judge who had referred to habeas proceedings as "S.O.B. jurisdiction," arguing that the biggest mistake Congress ever made was giving federal judges the right to review the learned decisions of state court judges. Only Ivey was optimistic.

"Judge Bowen is an honest jurist," he said. "He'll do the right thing."

At first it looked as if Ivey's prediction was, happily, the more accurate. Michael's petition for federal habeas relief was filed with the U.S. District Court for the Southern District of Georgia on January 24, 1986. A little over one year later, on February 17, 1987, Judge Bowen denied relief on all but two grounds—the confession issue and the conspiracy charge—and ordered an evidentiary hearing as to those two grounds. The wording of his prehearing order seemed to indicate quite clearly that he was leaning in Michael's favor as far as the confession issue was concerned. The conspiracy claim involved the prosecution's attempt to "attach the acts of the codefendant to Mr. Cervi . . . through a more sophisticated latterday conspiracy vehicle." Another, less appealing possibility was that he wanted to give the state a road map of what he needed in order to rule in their favor.

At the hearing on April 24, 1987 it was immediately apparent to Doyle that one of Judge Bowen's law clerks must have written his earlier order. Judge Bowen was not at all inclined to rule on Michael's behalf. Doyle quickly realized that the most he could accomplish at the hearing was to establish a good record for Michael's forthcoming appeal to the Eleventh Circuit. Once Doyle concluded that Judge Bowen was not on his side, his anxiety increased as he sat listening to the state's witnesses. Any one of them could have reached the same conclusion and added a critical fact.

In addition to eliciting crucial testimony to establish Michael's claim, Doyle had to ensure that there was no mention of anything that could hurt Michael. For instance, he had to be sure to preclude testimony about whether Michael had said anything that could have been construed as initiating the conversation with the Georgia authorities. Such a proactive move on Michael's part would have negated any constitutional violation. Since it was unclear whether Michael had, in fact, said anything of the sort, Doyle decided it was best to avoid the topic altogether. The Eleventh Circuit would thus be free to piece the confession together and would not be bound by an adverse factual finding. In retrospect, Doyle modestly contends that the self-discipline he mustered in not asking certain questions at the hearing was his greatest contribution to Michael's case. Ivey gives Doyle significantly more credit. "The record he managed to create was masterful," Ivey later said.

Judge Bowen ruled orally from the bench, leaving no room for hope.

> Accordingly it is my finding of fact and conclusion of law that the statement of Mr. Cervi was indeed admissible. It was not obtained by means of coercion or any other inappropriate means and after an evidentiary hearing on that subject matter area I find his conviction not to be in any way constitutionally infirmed because of its admission. Consequently I will enter a brief order, early next week, with reference to the finding and conclusion, given at the bench today, denying the writ and that will conclude the matter.

The one advantage to Judge Bowen's ruling at the hearing was that the attorneys had an opportunity to talk with Michael about the ruling immediately. Trying his best to put a positive spin on what was clearly a devastating blow for Michael, Doyle assured him that they had not lost any ground. "We have the record just the way we want it for the Eleventh Circuit," Doyle assured him. "We were able to protect what was already established in your favor, which was not a certainty, since Bowen's order granting the hearing gave the state plenty of hints about what they should do to make the record more favorable to them."

Ivey and Kendall joined in Doyle's optimistic predictions about how they would fare in the Eleventh Circuit. After all, they had each initially believed that Michael's best shot at relief lay with that court. But the nagging doubt they tried to hide from Michael was the realization that a good claim was only half the battle. They were hopeful, but also wary. They knew all too well that the Eleventh Circuit represented Michael's final shot at a legal remedy.

. . . .

While Doyle and Kendall were busy preparing the brief for the Eleventh Circuit, Ivey was busy with his own efforts at securing Michael's release. Ever since Michael's state appeals had proven futile, Ivey had been busy trying to sway public opinion in Michael's favor and come up with a creative means of reducing his sentence. He hoped to capitalize on the positive publicity and regard for Michael that he had generated following Michael's trial. The consensus in Taliafero County seemed to be that Michael had been excessively punished for his role in the crime, given that his codefendant, whom everyone viewed as the more culpable of the two, received only a life sentence.

Ivey approached the trial judge with a novel idea—one that only a local attorney with ties to the community could come up with, let alone implement. He was able to convince both the judge and the district attorney to let him approach each of the original jury members. If he could get them to unanimously agree to reduce Michael's sentence from death to life imprisonment, the court would sanction it. Over the years, Ivey tracked down the individual jury members and met with each one individually. The final count was ten in favor of reducing Michael's sentence, with two steadfastedly opposed. Even the district attorney, who had come to agree that Michael was worth saving, volunteered to meet with the jurors as a group. But the two holdouts refused to budge.

Michael nonetheless appreciated Ivey's efforts, and the fact that the judge and the district attorney were cooperating with Ivey was not lost on Michael. In a letter to Ivey, Michael acknowledged that "Mr. Goolsby and Judge Stevens are bending over backwards for me. I hope I can thank them in person."

Meanwhile, Michael's mother and brother were feeling increasingly helpless and hopeless in California:

> *Dear Mr. Ivey:*
>
> *Hello, again. We've finally accumulated enough money for another payment. Please find enclosed a check for $1,000. I hope all is going well with you. We are doing fine.*
>
> *I am writing to you this time because I don't want to worry my mother. However, several months ago, Mike mentioned his first federal appeal. We've been waiting optimistically for some good news. I haven't said anything to my mother, yet, but I can only assume once again we have been denied. This, of course, makes me very nervous. I'm sure had they taken the time to read your statement, they would have had to act. But it appears they read the State's side and ignore that of the defense.*
>
> *I really don't know what to do. I feel so helpless. This would be easier to take if it weren't such an obvious miscarriage of justice. I know you are just as frustrated. . . .*
>
> *Thanks for everything,*
> *Ron Cervi*

Not all of the changes brought about by Michael's incarceration were negative. While the entire family became extremely cynical about the nation's judicial system, they also became much more sympathetic to those individuals who suffered from its many injustices. Bernie Cervi, prior to his death, became far more compassionate about the criminals he had always taken pleasure in locking up. Juanita used to chide him that he would go to hell for the way he talked about some of the people he put behind bars. He had always referred to anyone so much as accused of a crime as undeserving of living, and he showed no sympathy for what family members of the accused endured. But armed with the unwelcome knowledge of what it was like to be a family member of someone who was locked up, Bernie's entire approach to his job changed. He began to see defendants as individuals deserving of a second chance, and he gave the families of criminals in his county much more latitude with respect to visitation and contact with their loved ones behind bars. He also grew increasingly religious, turning to his formerly lapsed faith as a means of dealing with both his and Michael's impending deaths. Juanita still finds some solace in realizing that Michael's horrible saga helped his father die a better man.

Ron, just a teenager when Michael was first arrested, also found his views altered by the experience. In a letter to Ivey prior to Michael's Eleventh Circuit appeal, he wrote:

> *All my life I've had such confidence in our judicial system. I was never even all that concerned about the legalization of the Death Penalty, because I figured with all the available appeals, only unsavory, habitual criminal characters would make it that far. We all know Mike doesn't fall into that category . . . the DA knew it, the judge knew it, even guards have told us Mike doesn't belong there. And yet appeal after appeal, we're being told Mike cannot be rehabilitated and would be a danger to society. This is the person convicted murderers go to for spiritual guidance.*

. . . .

William Boyd Tucker was one of Michael's best friends on Death Row. The two men had grown close during the five years they had been incarcerated together. Life in prison, viewed as a living hell by both men, was rendered more bearable by their mutual friendship. Even their mothers had become friends, having consoled each other during visits and through correspondence.

On May 27, 1987, Tucker called out a final good-bye to his buddy as he was escorted out of the cell block the two men shared. Tucker was on his way to the prison's Death House, located in Cell Block Five. He was scheduled to die in the prison's electric chair the next day.

Tucker was relatively composed as he left his fellow inmates and headed for his imminent death, but something in Michael snapped. He yelled out obscenities at the guards, infuriated that they were assisting in murdering his friend. Perhaps it was because Tucker's death made Michael's own death seem that much more inevitable, or perhaps it was because he had never had to stand by and await the execution of someone so close to him. For whatever reason, Michael knew that he had to act; he could not simply mourn his friend's death in silence and solitude.

It was common knowledge among the prisoners that an outside generator had to be brought into the prison whenever an execution took place, since the Georgia Power Company would not let Jackson use its electricity to kill people. Michael decided that his final gesture to his friend would be to blow up the generator. He knew this would buy Tucker only a few days at most, but he figured the courts would perhaps use the delay to reconsider Tucker's case and see the injustice of executing him. The knowledge of how unlikely it was that he would be able to reach the Death House and execute his plan did not deter Michael. Since he no longer had any faith in his own chances of prevailing in the courts, he assumed his day, too, would come. He decided he would rather be shot while pursuing something he believed in than die in the electric chair.

Michael wrote a letter to his mother telling her he loved her and apologizing for the pain he had caused her. He gave the letter to Tom Stevens, a fellow inmate and close friend.

"If I die tomorrow," Michael said. "Would you please mail this for me?"

Stevens at first tried to talk Michael out of his futile plan, but Michael was determined to carry it out. He accumulated several T-shirts and some matches, planning to climb the fence during the next day's recreational hour and, once he had made his way to the generator, stuff it with the T-shirts and set it on fire. Stevens was convinced that Michael would be shot before he even finished scaling the fence, and he did not want to see his friend die. Before Michael could leave his cell the following day, Stevens staged a fight with him so that they would both get locked up. The guards, however, knew that Michael and Stevens were friends and did not buy it. Instead, Michael was summoned to the captain's office, where he made something up about having insulted the Cleveland Browns, Stevens's favorite football team. The captain accepted Michael's explanation and simply admonished him not to pick fights in the future. Michael promptly gathered his things and ran into the yard before Stevens could again interfere with his plan.

Even though he was never shot, Michael was instantly sighted and kept within firing range of the prison's towers. He also had rifles aimed at him from the ground, where a truckload of officers were following his progress and yelling at him to come down. Michael was oblivious to the danger he was in, not to mention his pain from severely cutting himself on the barbed wire at the top of the wall and breaking his ankle when he jumped down from the wall onto the roof of the adjoining cell block. He was entirely focused on his mission, determined to get to the Death House and save his friend. Once he got there, however, he couldn't find the generator. It had not yet been brought into the prison. It was only then that Michael agreed to surrender, dropping down into an enclosed yard, where he was immediately subdued by dozens of officers.

Michael was charged with attempting to escape, for which he was sentenced to fifteen days in the hole. Even though he did not appeal the attempted escape charge, since he admittedly left the yard without permission, Michael wanted to make it clear that his motive had not been to escape. In a letter to the commissioner of the Department of Corrections appealing Michael's punishment, George Kendall noted that

> **[i]t strains reality to believe that anyone would attempt to escape on the day of an execution when security is tightened throughout the institution and when the area surrounding the institution is saturated with law enforcement personnel. Mr. Cervi wants you to know that his sole purpose for leaving the exercise area was to give aid to his close friend facing imminent execution.**

Michael was sentenced to an additional thirty days in the hole for injuring a correctional officer, a charge which he vehemently denied. The officer in question was injured when he was thrown from the truck as it followed Michael's progress on the ground. Both the warden and the superintendent of the Department of Corrections denied Michael's appeal, but the commissioner ultimately agreed that it was unfair to hold Michael responsible for an accident he in no way intended or caused.

The prison and the media nonetheless viewed Michael's efforts to save

Tucker as an attempted escape, which frustrated Michael more than the time he was serving for his efforts. As he stated in his letter to Commissioner Evans appealing the thirty-day sentence he received,

> Not only is this [the thirty-day sentence] unfair, but it is also deceitful. It is too convenient to convince the public and yourselves that a condemned killer tried to escape and an officer was injured in the process. This fits everybody's perception of a "mad dog killer." But that is not the truth! Is it so hard to believe that a man on death row can act virtuously? Do the fences and concrete keep nobility from coming within these walls? Narrow mindedness and bigotry have little to do with dispensing Justice. Don't let them infect your Department this way.

In a separate letter describing what he had done and what had motivated him, Michael explained,

> I know that purity of heart did Bill a lot of good after 2,000 volts passed into his brain. I believe that in faith. But as I stood on top of the death house, bleeding from cuts I received from the razor wire on the fences I had to climb, I could feel my leg throbbing as it swelled up on me as well. I could see the guards in the towers had me scoped in on their rifles, and scores were rapidly approaching on foot and by truck. The generator for the chair which I had come to blow up was nowhere to be seen. I could not get inside the death house to destroy the chair itself. My friend was going to die.
> There I was, one man alone, armed with two books of matches, and a heart full of courage. Hopelessly outnumbered, but fighting for a friend's life despite the odds. The only thing I had going for me was the conviction I was doing the right thing, a noble cause. Had I been fighting the "Japs" 40 years ago, I would have gotten a medal for the very same action. Now I get 45 days in the hole, and I'm told a brief bit in the paper: death row inmate tries to escape.
> Tuck, I know that purity of heart does you good "up there," but here it just got me in deep.

Michael also took issue with the local newspaper's account of what Ivey later referred to as his "First Amendment escape." Michael wrote a letter to the editor in an effort to dispel the public's "biased and preconceived notions of 'death row inmates,'" arguing that what he was trying to do "should come natural enough to anyone who has a son or daughter, brother or friend who was being threatened with death. As any decent friend would try to do for another, I was trying to save his life." As for his fellow Death Row inmates, Michael had this to say:

> *On the morning I was to make my attempt to destroy their killing machine, the one friend who I had told my plan tried to physically restrain me from going on the yard. He was sure the towers would open fire once I reached the roof. My life was, and is, important to him. Now that I'm in the hole, another friend got in trouble and was sent to the hole so he could keep me company.*
>
> *Such fidelity should be a welcome asset to any community. I give thanks to his Majesty that I have friends such as these.*

The only punishment Michael could not appeal, but found the hardest to endure, was his guilt over his failure to prevent Tucker's execution. At first, Michael continued to feel intense anger, viewing every guard and prison administrator as deserving of vengeance. His ire was soon replaced with total despair, and Michael felt himself succumbing to mental illness. What saved him were the efforts of people who cared about him, boosting his spirits not simply by their actions, but by the fact that they believed and supported him. Fellow inmate Andrew Lagare was the one who intentionally got into trouble so that he would be sent to the hole and could keep Michael company (he managed as well to sneak in some much-coveted cigarettes). George Kendall sent a paralegal to visit Michael regularly, since there were no limits on legal visits.

After Tucker's death, Juanita Cervi received a letter from Tucker's mother. "I hope you never have to go through what I just did," Mrs. Tucker wrote. "I don't wish this anguish on my worst enemies." For the first time, Juanita contemplated the possibility of losing her son. She had always comforted herself with Ivey's assurances that the state would never actually carry out Michael's death sentence, but now she was filled with doubt. Juanita had already buried a husband. She felt she could not endure another death.

. . . .

In the middle of the afternoon on August 26, 1988, Michael was summoned from his cell for a legal phone call. He knew his case was currently pending before the Eleventh Circuit, and he figured Kendall was probably just letting him know how things stood. His attorneys were diligent about keeping him updated and sharing every nuance of their legal battles on his behalf.

"We won, Mike!" Kendall exclaimed as soon as Michael picked up the phone. "We won!"

Michael responded to the news with exuberant screams.

"You there, Mike?" Kendall asked him. "You there?"

The order, issued that day, reversed the order of the district court and ordered a new trial. Circuit Judge R. Lanier Anderson held that the Georgia authorities had obtained Michael's confession in violation of his Fifth Amendment rights by initiating interrogation with him after he had requested counsel.

When Ivey got the news, he immediately called Ron and Juanita in California. Juanita knew it was good news because Ivey always wrote with the bad news, but called with the good. Even though Ivey had always assured her that Michael would not be executed, she realized then that she had never stopped worrying about it. Now, finally, she could.

After the state's request for a rehearing and a rehearing *en banc* (before the entire bench) was denied one month later, it applied to the U.S. Supreme Court for certiorari, which was also denied. It was only at that point that Michael was moved off Death Row, and he suddenly had the distinction of being the only happy inmate.

"What you got to be smiling about?" other inmates would grumble.

"Hey, I just got off of Death Row," Michael would say. "Life is good."

Indeed, Michael's entire attitude about his incarceration changed once his death sentence was lifted. Prior to the Eleventh Circuit's ruling, he had reached a point where he truly didn't care whether he lived or died, since he believed he was never going to get out of prison. The knowledge that he could now contemplate a life beyond the prison's walls changed his philosophy about doing time; he now had to show everyone that he was worthy of being released.

His new attitude was tested a few weeks later. A riot broke out in his cell block, which Michael would have probably joined prior to his turnaround. The inmates had blocked all the toilets to create a flood in protest of their horrible living conditions. When he was approached by his fellow inmates,

Michael told them he could no longer do those kinds of things. After placing all of his belongings on his bunk so that they would not get wet, Michael calmly sat in his cell and read a book while the riot took place around him. Even the guards were shocked.

"Cervi, why aren't you in on this?" they asked.

"I got too much to lose now," Michael answered.

. . . .

At first, both Michael and Ivey wanted to retry the case. They thought there was a good likelihood that Michael would actually be found not guilty. In the end, Kendall was able to convince them that the safer route would be to accept a guilty plea in exchange for more lenient sentencing. After all, if the case were retried, the death sentence remained an option, and it was simply too great a risk to take.

Now that the case was back in Taliaferro County, Ivey took over. In July 1989, he approached the district attorney with a plea agreement: Michael would plead guilty to all counts in exchange for two life sentences. This was a particularly good deal because it meant that Michael was immediately eligible for parole, having already served more than the requisite seven years. Ivey was able to avoid having Michael resentenced under the newer, stricter guidelines that would not have been as lenient.

Over the years, Ivey had been in contact with the parole board, sending them supplemental reports about Michael and his own account of Michael's alleged escape attempt. The parole board had written Michael a letter as soon as his sentence was overturned, indicating that they would consider his case within the next few years. Michael had actually met with them before, while he was on Death Row, but he had not distinguished himself during the interview. He longed to go before them again to plead his case, but they did not operate that way. Instead, they rendered a decision based on their review of each case file.

Michael was the first to learn he had been paroled. An inmate with whom he was friendly worked in the prison's front office, where he was able to see each day's incoming mail.

"Hey Cervi," he told Michael one day. "You got word from the parole board, and it's good news."

Two days later, Michael's counselor called him into his office and officially broke the news. After filling out all the paperwork and completing a parole plan, rendered somewhat more complicated because Michael wanted to return to California, Michael would be released.

The news caught everyone off guard. After hearing the good news from Michael, Juanita called Ivey to rave about what he had accomplished.

"I'd love to take credit for it," Ivey said. "But I didn't even know about it!"

Michael was released from prison on March 13, 1993, one day after his thirty-fifth birthday. He had been incarcerated for sixteen years. Juanita wanted to join Ron in flying out to bring Michael home, but Michael did not want her to come. The less she had to see of him in a prison context, the better.

Ron had a couple of Heinekens, Michael's favorite beer, waiting for him on the car seat. Michael also delved into the discarded day-old pizza slices sitting on the backseat of the car.

"Oh, man, don't eat that!" Ron exclaimed. "We'll go get you something good to eat."

But compared to prison fare, that stale pizza was a feast.

.　.　.　.　.　.　.　.

Prior to Michael's return home, Juanita's house had to pass muster with the parole board. She had to get rid of Bernie's extensive gun collection, since Michael could not live surrounded by so many weapons. Juanita wanted to protest to the gruff parole officer that her son was not a danger to society, but she was too happy about his coming home to jeopardize his parole in any way.

After the years in a prison cell, his mother's home seemed palatial to Michael. He also appreciated his surroundings, such as the view of San Francisco across the bay. Sitting in the house in the Hayward Hills and looking across the water to the San Francisco skyline was particularly meaningful to him; it was one of two visions that had sustained him during his incarceration. The other vision that Michael conjured up during particularly tough times was Cindy, whom he had never stopped loving. That vision, however, was one that Michael was not ready to confront in the flesh quite yet. For one thing, Ron had broken the news to him that Cindy had married in 1988. He was also unsure of how Cindy felt about him, given the way he had ended their relationship.

Cindy, meanwhile, had learned of Michael's release and was hurt that he did not try to contact her. She might have cared less if she had been happier in her marriage, but she and her husband, Jess, had grown distant. It was Jess who actually told her that Michael was back in town, wanting her to promise him that she would not initiate contact with him. Jess was threatened by Michael because Cindy had told him, before they were married, that the only two people she would ever contemplate having an affair with were Richard Gere and Michael. At the time, Michael was on Death Row with no prospect of getting out.

In August, five months after his release, Michael finally wrote to Cindy. He addressed the letter to her parents' home since he did not know her whereabouts. In his letter, Michael apologized for how he had ended things and assured her that he had never stopped thinking about her.

"I really want to see you," he wrote. "But I understand if you don't want anything to do with me." He promised her that he would not bother her again if he received no answer to his letter.

Cindy called Michael shortly after receiving his letter. They talked for a long time, and began to call each other regularly. Cindy was hesitant to see Michael, however, primarily because she felt self-conscious about her appearance, having just had a baby. Since Michael's efforts to convince her otherwise proved futile, he finally simply surprised her one day by showing up at her hairdresser's when she had let slip that she planned to get her hair cut that afternoon.

When she saw him standing there, waiting for her, Cindy went numb. She couldn't believe this tall, muscular man was Michael, and yet he was also so familiar. Cindy chastised Michael for surprising her, but it was clear she was as pleased to see him as he was to see her. They did nothing more than hug that afternoon, but both now look at that meeting as the beginning of their reunion.

Eventually, Cindy confided in Michael that her marriage was not going well and that Jess was verbally and physically abusive to her. One night in late 1993, she called Michael at 3:00 A.M., frantically telling him that Jess had just run her out of the house and that she had taken refuge at a neighbor's. She had tried calling her parents, but they were not home. Michael jumped in his car and rushed to Cindy's aid, arriving in time to see Jess chasing her down the street in her nightgown. Cindy had to physically restrain Michael from doing anything more than simply taking her home.

Cindy filed for divorce in December of 1993, but Jess refused to move out of the house. Michael finally moved in with Cindy and her son, Brendan, the following March. Cindy and Michael, who had originally been engaged in 1977, got married on January 20, 1994. Brendan, only two years old, immediately began calling Michael "Daddy" and considers him his father. Michael enjoys spending time with Brendan; he particularly likes teaching him about science and taking him to tae kwon do classes and tournaments. He is currently in the process of trying to legally adopt him. Michael and Cindy also have a daughter together, Lauren Michelle, who was born on August 27, 1994.

Cindy has accepted the fact that Michael committed the crime for which he was charged, but she still maintains that he was excessively punished for his role in the murder. Michael accepts responsibility for Dr. Lawrence's death and still struggles with the enormity of having ended another human being's life. On the other hand, he admits that those closest to him engender more of his remorse; he is more concerned with the pain and suffering he caused his own family than that suffered by Dr. Lawrence and his family.

Michael is also uneasy with the distinction of having been released when several friends of his whose cases were even more compelling were executed or continue to serve out sentences. He occasionally takes a few Heinekens to his favorite spot on a hill overlooking the San Francisco Bay and toasts his old buddies as well as his own good fortune. He continues to correspond with some of the men who remained behind, although Cindy feels uneasy about some of the requests made of her husband and the guilt he clearly feels about his freedom.

One of the things Michael has confessed to those who are still locked up is that life on the outside is not always easy. His only work experience since his release was with a friend who owned a small construction company, but there is no longer enough work to justify keeping Michael on the payroll. He has gone back to school to get a college degree, but the administration recently found out about his past and has made life difficult for him. He has also been shunned at job interviews, leaving him convinced that the only way he will get hired is to say "no" in response to the standard application question, "Have you ever been convicted of a crime?"

The legal system is satisfied that Michael has paid for his crime, but that has not translated into societal forgiveness and acceptance.

judy haney

Judy Haney is not a morning person, but she arises every morning at 5:00 A.M. By 7:00, she has had breakfast and is at her job in the sewing factory. Her regimented day continues with lunch at 11:00 a.m, followed by another work shift until 4:00 P.M. Dinner is eaten at 4:30 every afternoon, after which she is free to do what she likes until bedtime. Her recreational options are limited, however, because Judy is an inmate at Tutwiler Women's Prison in Wetumpka, Alabama. She may opt to walk around the fenced-in yard, or she may read or write a letter. Sometimes she washes herself in the communal showers, which are turned on from 2:30 until 5:30 A.M. and again from 3:30 until 9:00 P.M.

Judy wears an all-white uniform that is snug on her large frame. She has to make special requests for brassieres that offer her the support she needs for her ample chest. Her hair has changed color from a deficiency in her diet, and most of her teeth will be removed shortly because they have rotted from a lack of hygiene. Sleep is sought each night on a small bed lined up with a hundred other beds in a cramped dormitory in Tutwiler's medium security facility. The prison houses a total of 700 female inmates, 24 of whom are, like Judy, sentenced to life without the possibility of parole.

It is not the life Judy envisioned for herself as a young girl in Talladega, Alabama. Her childhood dream was to get married, have kids, and live in a large house in the country. Much of what Judy wished had come true. She married Jerry Haney in January 1968, at the age of sixteen, and gave birth to a daughter, Tonya, and a son, Gary. She and Jerry bought their own home which, while smaller than her dream house, was not far from where she grew up and had a barn and horses in the back. Her abusive husband, however, was not at all like the one of her dreams. Just as Judy never imagined herself spending the remainder of her days behind bars, she never anticipated the hell that was her marriage.

. . . .

Haney was born Judy Milstead on June 29, 1951, in Rome, Georgia. Her first twelve years were spent in a nomadic trek across the South, uprooted each time her father, a millwright, moved to a different state to set up looms in new factories. In 1964, the Milsteads moved to Talladega County, Alabama, and decided to stay. Judy and her siblings (a span of twenty-three years separated the oldest from the youngest) were happy to settle down. The two oldest, Betty and Linda, had married and moved out of the house, making Judy the second-oldest of the four who remained at home.

Judy's father was a weekend drunk, which served to exacerbate his already volatile temper. However, he was not the one who inspired fear in his children, since he was the type of man who "wore the pants in the family when the missus wasn't around." It was Judy's mother who set down the rules and meted out the punishments; her word was law. Her most frequent form of punishment was to whip her children, and Judy was no exception. One lesson she impressed upon her daughters above all others was the consequences of sexual relations prior to marriage.

"If you have sex with a boy, you instantly get pregnant," Mrs. Milstead told her girls. "And if you get pregnant, I'll kill you."

Judy believed her mother with all her heart and was not even tempted to disobey her. That is not to say that she did not have feelings of passion or fantasies about what sex would be like, but she knew that pursuing sexual relations before a trip to the altar was akin to suicide.

By the time she was sixteen, Judy dropped out of school. She had already failed the seventh grade, having attended seven or eight different schools in that year alone. She then completed eighth and ninth grades in Talladega County before quitting school entirely. Her older sister, Martha, had already dropped out, so Judy simply followed in her footsteps. She spent her days working in the garden or taking long walks on the winding country roads surrounding her house. Her mother didn't care or supervise what she did as long as she stayed out of her hair.

Jerry Haney and his family moved in next door to the Milsteads in October 1967. Donald Haney, Jerry's oldest brother, wasted no time in asking Judy out on a date, but she declined. He warned her that his younger brother, Jerry, was crazy, but to sixteen-year-old Judy, that made Jerry all the more appealing. When Jerry asked her out one month later, she agreed to a date. She actually felt sorry for the pimple-faced boy, one year her senior, who worked the third shift (11:00 P.M. to 7:00 A.M.) at a local bag manufacturer. Jerry was recovering from a shotgun blast to his back at the hand of his father; rumor had it that it had not been an accident. Jerry and Judy dated for only a couple of months before deciding to wed, which they did in January 1968.

Looking back on her courtship, Judy cannot remember feelings of love or fantasies of what married life would be like. She attributes her hasty and early marriage to the simple fact that she had to be Jerry's wife before she could leave home. She was desperate to get away from her parents' rule and their chaotic home.

The young couple lived with the Haneys for a few weeks, but Judy complained that it was simply too crowded and there was never enough food to eat. They then moved in with her family, but were kicked out four months later when Jerry had a fight with Judy's brother. By then, Jerry could afford to rent a small house in the country, right up the road from his cousin Ernestine.

Married life was initially not very different from Judy's life at her parents' house. Jerry did not want her to work, demanding instead that she keep their small rental house clean, tend to his horse, and have food on the table each night upon his return. The last proved to be a challenge for Judy. The first meal she prepared for her husband was a complete disaster, particularly since she had bragged to him while they were dating that she was as good a cook as her mother, whose skills in the kitchen were legendary.

"The pork chops were so tough you couldn't hardly chew through them," Judy recalls. "The beans weren't cooked enough, and I didn't know to put any seasoning on them, and the greens weren't washed so they had little black bugs all over them. And the biscuits were so hard you could have had a ball game with them for months."

Jerry took one look at the bounty Judy had proudly served and demanded some bologna.

"I'll make my own damn sandwich," he growled, when Judy got up to get him some. "You've done enough damage."

The next day he hauled Judy over to her mother's house and demanded that his mother-in-law teach his wife how to cook.

As Judy's housekeeping and cooking skills increased, so did Jerry's expectations of perfection. He inspected everything, insisting that Judy do things a certain way. The bedspread could not have any wrinkles; the towels had to be lined up just so; and his horse had to be cleaned and fed according to his specifications. Any perceived deviation incurred his wrath. He also became increasingly possessive and domineering. He insisted that Judy remain isolated in their country house, and severely restricted her contact with her family and friends. He particularly forbade her visiting Ernestine, even though she was their closest neighbor.

The first time Judy felt real fear of her husband and his temper was when she was seven months pregnant with Tonya. Ernestine, whom Judy had continued to see on a daily basis despite Jerry's warnings, had pierced Judy's ears that day. Judy thought maybe Jerry wouldn't notice the small blue baubles that made her feel so special, but he saw them immediately.

"What's that in your ears?" he asked.

"Ernestine pierced my ears today," Judy replied, trying to remain calm.

Jerry knocked the earring through her ear so that it came out on the opposite side. As she bled profusely, he made sure she understood that disobeying him was dangerous business.

"If Ernestine ever comes back," he yelled, "I'll kill you."

Judy was terrified. Jerry had hit her before, but not like this, and not when she was seven months pregnant with their first child. When Ernestine showed up the next day, Judy told her she had to leave. Ernestine urged Judy to tell her parents, but Judy knew better. If she told, her father would kill Jerry for sure. At the time, she still loved her husband. He was, after all, the father of the child growing inside of her. She couldn't tell her parents.

The next month, Jerry's twelve-year-old brother, Billy, moved in with them. Billy did not yet know how exacting his brother was, but he learned the hard way shortly after he arrived. Upset that Billy had not fed his horse properly, Jerry followed him out to the pasture and beat him mercilessly. Judy ran out in time to intercept a metal bucket Jerry had thrown at his little brother, which sliced open her thigh in a three-inch gash that bled profusely. Jerry opted to wrap the cut at home rather than take her to the emergency room for stitches. He did not yet realize, as he would over time, that Judy was too afraid and embarrassed to disclose to others how she had sustained her injuries in response to the inevitable queries about what had happened. As was his norm, Jerry became extremely apologetic after his fit of rage, promising never to hurt Judy again.

Visits to her in-laws gave Judy insight into why Jerry treated her the way he did, but did not provide any solutions for ending the cycle of violence. Jerry's father routinely beat his mother, prompting Mrs. Haney to occasionally resort to faking a heart attack in order to get him to stop. Judy, a large, strong woman who had fought with her own siblings throughout her childhood, initially slapped and kicked back when Jerry beat her. Once, when she anticipated a particularly bad beating, she armed herself with a butcher's knife and locked herself and the kids in her bedroom. Jerry, all the more enraged because he'd had to break down the door, broke her nose and ribs. Judy tried to stab him with the knife, but it merely bounced off his ribs.

"Oh, you're a stupid bitch," Jerry said, incredulous that she had fought back.

He ended up taking her to the hospital that night, and Judy concluded that fighting back only made things worse. She decided to emulate her mother-in-law and simply endure the Haney abuse.

Judy tried to make everything in Jerry's life perfect so that he would have less cause to beat her. When he was at work, however, she operated under the premise that what her husband didn't know wouldn't hurt him. If she had done as Jerry wished, she would have never left her home except to go to work. Jerry tolerated her working at the local sewing factory because it enabled them to buy their own home. It was Judy's salary that paid for their new furniture, their new truck, and all their brand-new appliances. Jerry's earnings went to his two show horses and their requisite trailers, food, and equipment.

Over the years, Jerry placed increasingly severe limitations on Judy's contact with her family. Her parents had moved to Georgia when Tonya was a baby, and Judy was allowed to visit them only once each year, for Christmas. Jerry would drive his family to the Milstead home on Christmas Eve and then insist that they leave the following day. Judy's siblings were not allowed to visit her, nor she them.

When her mother's health declined, and she was in and out of the hospital for two years, Judy repeatedly begged to be able to visit her, to no avail. When her mother's death seemed imminent and Judy's sisters began a round-the-clock vigil at her hospital bed, Judy decided she was going to go, no matter what. She arranged for someone to watch the children and packed them into the car in the hope of heading out before Jerry returned from work. She didn't make it.

"Where you think you're going, bitch?" he demanded.

"My mama's dying, and I've got to be there," Judy replied. "Barbara's going to watch the kids and everything is all set."

"Oh, no it ain't," Jerry said, in that steely voice that ensured he meant business. "You ain't goin' nowhere."

Judy, at her most determined, started out the door despite his threats. She ended up with a broken nose and punctured sinuses, which caused severe hemorrhaging.

Jerry dropped the kids off at his brother Billy's house before rushing Judy to the emergency room.

"My God, Jerry," Billy gasped, eyeing his bloody sister-in-law crumpled in the front seat. "Can't you keep your damn hands to yourself?"

At the hospital, Dr. Lambert, who had seen Judy on prior occasions, asked her what had happened.

"I ran into a brick wall," Judy muttered.

"Well, I tell you what," Dr. Lambert replied. "That brick wall is going to kill you if you don't get the hell away from it."

Judy's entire face swelled and turned black with blood and bruising. Her eyes were sealed shut, her nose was packed to repair the damage, and she was given heavy pain medications. By the time she was well enough to travel, her mother had died.

. . . .

Jerry's beatings were not limited to his wife, although she incurred the worst of his abuse. He once broke Tonya's arm, and he often beat Gary with his belt and even tried to choke him on one occasion. Judy would always intercede to protect her kids, knowing that an even more enraged man would then vent his anger on her. His biggest gripe, however, resulting in the worst beatings, was his constant but ungrounded fear that Judy was having an affair. Even harmless greetings to the local cops, all of whom knew Judy because her brother-in-law Billy was on the force, always seemed to get back to Jerry. Judy could not for the life of her figure out the source of Jerry's information until one of the cops clued her in to the fact that her so-called best friend, Louise, was having an affair with her husband.

For Judy, the fact that Jerry, who was always accusing her of fooling around behind his back, was unfaithful himself served as the final straw. She snuck over to the church parking lot, where she had been told they rendezvoused, and saw Jerry's truck there, confirming that the affair was, in fact, going on. She then let the air out of Jerry's tires, hiding out long enough to see him return in Louise's car and rage about "the damn niggers" who had vandalized his truck.

Judy returned to the house and packed up all of her belongings. She already had the children in the car and was heading out the door when Jerry returned.

"What the hell's going on?" he bellowed, noting the packed car.

"I'm getting the hell out of here," Judy yelled back. "I know about you and Louise. The gig's up."

"Bitch, you ain't going nowhere," Jerry said, slapping her hard on the cheek.

"Slap the other side, you motherfucker," Judy cried, turning her cheek. "Because it's the last time you're ever going to hit me."

After Jerry slapped her again, Judy managed to run to the car, where her terrified children awaited her. As she struggled to start the car, Jerry had lifted the hood and was endeavoring to pull out the electrical wires.

"You'll have to run me over, bitch," he yelled. "'Cause I ain't moving."

"Fine by me," Judy replied, revving the motor. Jerry moved out of the way just in time.

Judy went straight to Linda and Billy's house, Jerry's brother and sister-in-law. Judy was close to Linda, and both Linda and Billy had seen first-hand the abuse she had suffered. She and the children lived in a trailer in Linda and Billy's backyard from October until December 1983. Jerry visited often, full of apologies for the way he had treated Judy and imploring her to give him another chance.

In December, in a gesture intended to show her what a changed man he was, Jerry offered to swap living space with Judy and the kids. Judy, Tonya, and Gary moved back into the house, and Jerry moved into the trailer. Judy still did not trust him, however, so she had the locks changed. Sure enough, Jerry returned that night and was livid that he couldn't get into his own house. He beat on the door and cursed her until Judy called Billy and told him to "come pick up [his] sorry ass brother" before she called the cops.

By Christmas, Judy had agreed to let Jerry stay over so that they could enjoy the holidays as a family. She insisted on separate bedrooms, however, despite Jerry's assurances that his affair was over and that he was totally devoted to Judy and their marriage.

"That motherfucker can have everything," she decided. "I don't want to fight anymore. I'll just get the hell out of Dodge."

If Judy had any doubts about leaving everything behind, the next day's beating convinced her. She heard hollering down by the barn, and ran down to discover her supposedly reformed husband "beating the shit out of the kids." Tonya and Gary, both slight for their ages, had accidentally dropped the fifty-pound feed bag that their father had ordered them to bring down to the barn. When Judy intercepted him, he turned on her and began choking her. It was only with both children jumping on him that he let go, but not before leaving bruises in the shape of his hands across her neck. When Jerry relented, it was not to apologize, as he customarily did after a beating, but instead to stare at his family in hatred and fury.

"I ain't done with you," Jerry said in a tone that alarmed Judy.

He shoved his family into the barn and locked them in, warning them that he'd be back that night to finish giving them what they deserved.

As soon as Jerry was gone, Judy hoisted Tonya up to the barn window. "Run up to the house as fast as you can and call Aunt Martha," Judy instructed her daughter. "Tell her to come get us." Martha was Judy's sister who was closest to her in age; she lived in nearby Calhoun, Georgia. When Martha picked up the phone, she could barely understand her frantic niece.

"Mama and Daddy had a big, bad fight," Tonya gasped. "Come get us. Hurry up."

Before Martha could ask any questions or assure Tonya that she was on her way, Tonya added, "He's going to kill us this time for sure."

. . . .

Tonya was right about someone getting killed, but that someone was not her mother, as she had feared. On January 1, 1984, Jerry Haney was shot in the stomach with a shotgun. He was shot again while he was on the ground, having been knocked down by the first blast, but he managed to get up and run off of the front porch of his house and around a hedge.

Judy learned of her husband's death from his brother Billy; she had asked him to go check on Jerry when he failed to answer her repeated phone calls the following morning. It was Billy who discovered his brother's body, rendered nearly unidentifiable from the blast that obliterated much of his face. The gunshot wound to his mouth is what killed Jerry, as reported by the Alabama Department of Forensic Sciences after they conducted an autopsy. The final shotgun blast "fractured almost every bone in the victim's skull, fractured the first two cervical vertebrae, and drove a tooth into Haney's spinal cord." The fact that Jerry Haney was brutally murdered is uncontestable. What is not as clear, and continues to be a matter of debate, is his wife's role in his death.

Judy maintains that Jerry called shortly after she arrived at Martha and

Jerry Henderson's house in Calhoun, Georgia, on December 31, 1983. He threatened to kill her if she did not immediately return.

"You'd better get home," Jerry said. "Or I'm going to come up there and drag you back to Alabama."

Both Tonya and Judy were crying hysterically after hanging up the phone. Judy didn't know what to do. She and her sister and brother-in-law sat down to discuss Judy's situation.

There are several different accounts of what was discussed and what transpired as a result of the discussion. Among the few points on which Judy and the Hendersons agree is that Judy gave her brother-in-law directions on how to get to her house, since Jerry Henderson had never been there before. In fact, Judy had met her brother-in-law on only two prior occasions, at each of her parents' funerals. She did not know him well at all, and she was unaware that he had a criminal record for armed robbery. And despite what may or may not have been said at the time, Judy has always sworn that she did not believe Jerry Henderson would actually go to Talladega to kill her husband.

What is irrefutable is that Jerry Henderson, while he and his wife were entertaining friends on New Year's night, 1984, claimed he had the flu and retired to his bedroom. It is also uncontested that he returned home from Alabama at 3:30 the next morning and presented Judy with her husband's flashlight and his billfold.

"He's dead," Jerry Henderson said. "You never have to worry about that S.O.B. hurting you or the kids again."

Judy maintains that she never asked or expected her brother-in-law to murder her husband, even though she wanted Jerry out of her life. In fact, she did not even believe Henderson when he informed her of her husband's death. Later that morning, Judy tried repeatedly to call her home. She assumed that Henderson had knocked Jerry unconscious and that was why her husband was not answering the phone. He could not possibly be dead. She finally resorted to calling Jerry's brother, Billy.

"Where is that damn brother of yours?" she asked. "Go check if he's at the barn."

Judy finally called Billy back at 12:30 P.M. Billy's stepdaughter answered the phone, but hung up when she heard Judy on the line. Judy got a sickening feeling in her stomach. Something was definitely wrong.

At 2:00 P.M., Billy called Martha. Judy heard her sister say, "I'm sorry. I'll tell her."

"He's dead," Martha told Judy when she hung up the phone, and this time Judy knew it was true.

Judy maintains that her brother-in-law informed her he'd hired a hit man, and that she needed to come up with $3,000 and keep her mouth shut. Jerry Henderson threatened that the hit man would "wipe out" all of them if Judy did not pay up. Judy had no intention of paying Henderson the $3,000, since she assumed the hit man story was merely his attempt to profit from the murder. By June, however, she became convinced of the hit man's existence. Tonya called her at work one day in a panic to report that a man with a shotgun had shown up in their backyard and threatened her. Judy recalls that when Billy investigated, at her behest, he found footprints in the backyard.

"You've got to fork over the $3,000 you owe," Henderson told her when she called him to report the unidentified man, "or he will kill us all."

By August, Judy had obtained a home improvement loan and paid Henderson the money. She didn't know for sure whether he was keeping the money or not, but she couldn't risk ignoring his account of a hit man.

To this day, Judy does not know whether the murderer was her brother-in-law or someone he hired. She only knows that she neither murdered her husband nor hired her brother-in-law to kill him. Her crime, which she wishes she had simply confessed to when first interrogated by the police, was paying for Jerry's murder after the fact.

The police were convinced that Judy had hired her husband's killer, and they repeatedly questioned her about it. But Judy stood by her story that she knew nothing about the murder, and they simply had no evidence against her. She continued to be employed and raise her two children. The case might have been abandoned were it not for the single-minded pursuit of state investigator Dennis Surrett, who pursued Judy with the same determination and obstinacy with which Inspector Javert sought Jean Valjean in *Les Misérables*.

The break that Surrett was waiting for came in the fall of 1987, when Martha Henderson agreed to turn state's evidence. She and Jerry Henderson had separated, and Martha had been picked up with her new boyfriend for possession of cocaine. She agreed to assist the police in nabbing both Judy and her ex-husband, whom they had always suspected, in exchange for leniency on the drug charges as well as her own involvement in Jerry Haney's death.

When Martha called Judy out of the blue in September 1987, Judy instantly interpreted the call as a setup. The two sisters had had little contact since the payoff, and it struck Judy as odd that Martha was trying to engage her in a conversation about the crime.

"You must be on drugs," Judy repeatedly said in response. "I don't know what the hell you're talking about."

A few days later, Martha showed up unannounced at Judy's house. Again, Judy smelled a setup. Despite the ninety-degree temperature that day, Martha was wearing a coat. She refused to take it off, and continued to try unsuccessfully to discuss Jerry's murder with Judy. While they were talking, Judy grabbed a piece of cardboard and wrote on it, "Marty, I know you're wired. The gig's up." Upon reading what her sister had written, Martha turned white and ran out of the house.

Martha had more luck with her ex-husband. On September 9, 1987, she managed to discuss the case with Henderson by phone from the backseat of her car, recording every word on tape. Henderson was arrested on September 12, 1987, and confessed to the capital murder of his brother-in-law the following day. In his confession, Henderson claimed that Judy hired him to murder her husband. She was arrested that same day and charged with murder for hire and murder committed during a robbery in the first degree. The arrests allowed the police to finally close a case that had remained unsolved for nearly four years.

. . . .

Gould H. K. Blair was appointed by this Court as Co-Counsel to represent the defendant, Judy M. Haney in the case of State of Alabama v. Judy M. Haney, a capital murder case. At around 9:30 A.M. during the trial of said case and while the Court was in session, the Court observed Attorney Blair conducting himself in a bizarre manner. His speech was slow and slightly slurred, his walking movements were unstable and his facial appearance was flushed and his eyes were reddened. In attempting to read a code section to the Court, Attorney Blair had to shut one eye, which was completely out of the ordinary for him.

On October 20, 1988, Gould H. K. Blair was found in contempt of court and incarcerated until the following day after Judge Jerry Fielding concluded that he was intoxicated in court. Once Blair returned to the courtroom, he hardly opened his mouth. "It was as if they had told him to shut up," Judy recalls. On the few occasions that she met with him (twice prior to the start of trial), she noticed that he seemed to eat a steady stream of Tic Tacs. Blair's "drinking incident," as he later referred to it, was not the only way in which he and his cocounsel, William Denson, let Judy down (Blair insisted that the incident in no way undermined Judy's defense).

The thrust of Judy's defense was that she lacked the necessary intent to commit the crime because her judgment was impaired by "spouse abuse syndrome" and fear of her husband. This approach, already risky because there was both time and distance separating Judy from the murder, was rendered even more challenging because of Blair's and Denson's ineptitude. They failed to obtain an expert to testify on Judy's behalf until after the trial had started. They neglected to interview and call as witnesses any of her friends and colleagues who could have corroborated her account of the abuse she had suffered. They did not obtain the medical records from the hospital where Judy was treated for her injuries, because they had not even subpoenaed them until two days before the trial. And they never subpoenaed the doctors and nurses who had treated Judy and who could have refuted the state's claim that Judy was lying about suffering spousal abuse when the hospital's custodian of records testified that no such medical records could be found. (The records were miraculously unearthed *after* Judy's sentencing.) Blair and Denson failed to adequately educate the court about the nature of being a battered wife and the fact that Judy's size and physical condition had no bearing on whether she had been abused. And they failed Judy, as did the legal system, because they let a woman who had suffered fifteen years of abuse from a man (who was not a likeable victim by anyone's standards) receive the death penalty for a crime she continues to maintain she did not commit.

Judy had always believed in and respected the American judicial system. Her only prior legal infractions had been writing some bad checks for groceries, an electric bill, and a car payment when she was awaiting a workers' compensation check. In fact, when she was arrested at work for the bounced checks, she was sure it was because of the murder. Judy was extremely regretful that she had not come forward with the full extent of her involvement when the police had first questioned her. She nonetheless assumed that the state's pursuit of the death penalty in her case was a means of scaring her rather than an actual threat. Even if the jury accepted the state's characterization of Judy's role in Jerry's murder, it was still unlikely that they would sentence her to death for such a crime. When they did on October 24, 1988, she was completely shocked.

"You could have knocked me over with a feather," she recalls with her customary sense of humor, "and I'm a big girl!"

. . . .

Despite his contempt citation for appearing drunk in court and his inadequate handling of Judy's case at trial, Gould Blair was nonetheless appointed by the court to handle Judy's case on direct appeal. Judy asked him whether he had ever handled a capital case before, and as she later described his response, "he beat around the bush and said he had helped on another appeal." She tried calling him once from prison because some attorneys had asked her to testify in a civil case involving someone she knew, but he would not accept the phone charges and told her to write to him instead. He also refused to send her a copy of the trial transcript, explaining that she would not be able to understand it because she was not a lawyer.

Judy knew she deserved better. She filed a complaint with the Alabama bar, citing Blair's many failings and requesting new counsel. Blair accused her of ruining his career and said she was a lying and conniving woman.

"I am through with handling your case as of today," he said, before she hung up on him.

The Alabama Resource Center, now known as the Equal Justice Initiative, got involved and agreed to try to find Judy a new attorney. In early 1990, they contacted the Southern Center for Human Rights, which agreed to take over the case. It was assigned to Charlotta Norby.

Norby first came to the United States from Denmark as an au pair. She then stayed on in Georgia, attending Georgia State University as an undergraduate and majoring in criminal justice. In the course of a student internship doing death penalty work, she was introduced to Stephen Bright and the Southern Center for Human Rights. By then Norby knew that she wanted to do death penalty defense work, and she attended New York University Law School with that goal in mind. She used her scholarship money to return to Atlanta during her first two summers and worked as a volunteer at the center. Bright did not have the funds, however, to hire her upon her graduation from law school the following year, so she worked instead as a clinical fellow in the Criminal Justice Clinic at Georgetown

University Law Center for two years. She was finally able to join the Southern Center's small staff of attorneys the following year, having secured her own funding through a Skadden Arps Fellowship. By the time her fellowship expired, Bright had raised enough money to hire her on a permanent basis.

At the point that Norby received the case, Blair had already missed two statutorily imposed deadlines for filing a brief to the Alabama Court of Criminal Appeals. Having lost a motion for a new trial, he did not appeal the ruling to Alabama's Court of Criminal Appeals, as he was required to do. Nor had he requested more time in which to do so. Norby did not even bother to file a motion to remove Blair from the case, since it was clear he was not doing anything as Judy's attorney. After she filed her appellate brief, however, having requested and been granted extra time in which to do so, Blair filed one as well. When Norby argued the case before the Court of Criminal Appeals, she was asked by the court what they should do about Blair's brief.

"Ignore it," Norby responded, having looked it over and concluded it had absolutely nothing of value to add. "I now represent Ms. Haney."

The court did ignore it, as requested, but nonetheless subsequently approved Blair's voucher requesting payment for his efforts in writing it.

Norby was successful in getting the case remanded, but not for the reasons she had anticipated. In fact, she lost on every issue she raised except the narrow one involving the court's consideration of a victim impact statement in the sentencing phase of the trial. The statement, included as part of the standard presentence investigation report provided by the court probation and parole officer, "described the emotional impact of the crimes on the victim's family and set forth the family members' opinions and characterizations of the crimes and appellant." Since the Alabama Court of Criminal Appeals could not presume that the trial court had disregarded the statement, deemed a "constitutionally unacceptable risk" by the U.S. Supreme Court in *Booth v. Maryland*, it remanded the case to the trial court "with instructions to resentence appellant, without considering the victim impact statement, and issue new written findings."

Norby instantly filed a motion requesting that the court reconsider all of the other issues that she had raised. On a Monday, the Court of Appeals instructed her and Bright that they would have to wait to file any such motions until after the remand was decided. On the following Wednesday afternoon, they were informed by the trial court that the new sentencing hearing would take place that Friday at 1:00 P.M. Bright moved to be admitted pro hac vice and immediately wrote a motion requesting more time in which to prepare and subpoena witnesses, which he filed with the court on Friday morning. The judge refused to allow him to argue the motion, however, since he was not a member of the Alabama bar. Norby, completely unprepared since she had counted on Bright to make the arguments, had to keep asking him what to say. She finally succeeded in obtaining a continuance until the following Monday. It accomplished little as far as providing sufficient time to track down defense witnesses, but it at least provided an opportunity to obtain pro hac vice status for Bright, enabling him to argue the case when it resumed.

In Alabama, even when a jury unanimously agrees on a defendant's sentence, the case nonetheless goes to the trial judge after the jury's determination. The judge can disregard the jury's ruling. In Judy's case, the jury had ruled 10 to 2 in favor of imposing a death sentence. Judge Jerry Fielding, who had presided over Judy's trial in the Talladega County Circuit Court, had then sentenced Judy to death. On remand, Judge Fielding did so again. It was clear he viewed the remand as requiring him to do nothing more than retype his order with the omission of the victim impact statement that was erroneously included in the first presentence report. Left with no time in which to track down any witnesses, Bright and Norby were unable to present any. When the judge retired to consider Judy's fate for a second time, he was essentially armed with nothing different from the first time, other than the absence of the victim impact statement. He returned with a verdict before Norby and Bright had even left the courtroom.

"Good luck, Miss Haney," Judge Fielding said, having just sentenced her to death again.

"Good luck with what?" Norby thought to herself. "With your appeals? With dying?"

. . . .

Norby and Bright returned to Atlanta and immediately filed a notice of appeal from the new death sentence. Before they had even had an opportunity to write the accompanying brief, the Alabama Court of Criminal Appeals affirmed the sentence of death.

"But you haven't even seen the transcript yet," Bright and Norby wrote in protest. "We haven't even submitted our brief."

The Court of Criminal Appeals agreed to wait until it received the transcript. But on March 29, 1991, again without the benefit of Norby and Bright's brief, the court denied a rehearing and affirmed the death sentence. Norby and Bright next appealed to the Alabama Supreme Court, which affirmed the judgment of the Court of Criminal Appeals on June 19, 1992. The two attorneys then petitioned the U.S. Supreme Court for certiorari, focusing on the issue of whether an accomplice should be held liable for the statutory aggravating circumstances (the heinous way in which Jerry Haney had been murdered) if she did not carry out the murder herself. Certiorari was denied on February 22, 1993.

Norby and Bright began seeking volunteers to take over the case. Other cases and clients demanded their attention, and they knew Judy's case would be an easy sell. Convinced the case would appeal to women's rights advocates, they contacted the Battered Women's Task Force and were put in touch with an attorney named Christine Andriolli, who agreed to take over the case. At the time, Andriolli was working at the New York law firm of Kaye, Scholer, Fierman, Hays, and Handler, which had a strong commitment to pro bono work and to death penalty cases in particular. Kaye, Scholer immediately recruited a team of associates to work on the case with Andriolli, among them a fourth-year associate named John Geelan.

As a civil litigator whose clients were large corporations, Geelan had little expertise to offer. He had just handled his first pro bono murder case, and he was reluctant to get involved in another all-consuming pro bono matter. He was also leery about pushing his luck, since he had succeeded in getting the attempted murder conviction of his previous client overturned and knew such outcomes were rare.

"I'll help," he told the assigning partner. "But I don't want to play a major role."

Geelan soon changed his mind, however. Once he read the transcript, he became angry and eager to rectify the injustice Judy had suffered. His decision to become more involved in the case was also prompted by Andriolli's departure from the firm shortly after agreeing to take it on. That left Geelan and Dave Pegno, another attorney whom Andriolli had recruited. Pegno was the lead counsel, but when he left Kaye, Scholer the following year, Geelan became the lead counsel on the case. In the three years that he represented Judy, he logged an average of 500 to 700 hours per year on her case alone. At the time, his hourly rate as a fifth-year associate was approximately $240 per hour.

Geelan's first order of business was to file the state habeas petition. He did so one month before the filing deadline, because he didn't want the case to move forward too quickly. He needed as much time as possible to gather the necessary evidence, and he knew that as long as the case was alive, so was his client. Unlike his other civil cases, where a loss was measured in financial terms, losing Judy's case would result in her death.

The state of Alabama promptly moved to dismiss the petition, which prompted Geelan to fly down to Talladega County to meet with the judge and the attorney from the Alabama attorney general's office who was handling the case. Geelan agreed to file an amended petition that addressed the concerns the state raised regarding the specificity of his claims as well as issues of timing. The judge then ruled on the amended petition, dismissing all of the claims except those dealing with ineffective assistance of counsel and violations of *Brady v. Maryland*. A *Brady* claim essentially argues that the prosecution did not disclose exculpatory evidence and that the defense was disadvantaged by the missing evidence. The ineffective assistance of counsel claim essentially focused on the failure of Judy's trial counsel to obtain evidence of the severe battering that Judy suffered at the hands of her husband.

Geelan worked closely on the case with Kelly Lawson, another Kaye, Scholer associate. Geelan, Lawson, and the rest of the Kaye, Scholer team (which included Beth Rodgers, Juan Ordonez, Catherine Barofsky, Lori Leskin, John Howley, and David Soskin) began the discovery process, in which they collected, identified, and examined the evidence and witnesses, which should have been done for Judy's initial trial. Geelan began to feel that both of their claims showed great promise. Accompanied by two other attorneys from Kaye, Scholer, who were also devoting hundreds of billable hours to the pro bono case, Geelan and Lawson set up shop in Alabama and conducted a full-blown investigation of Judy's case.

With Judy's assistance, the Kaye, Scholer team was able to track down and interview over seventy witnesses. It was not until Geelan and Lawson started questioning the witnesses, many of them former colleagues of Judy's at the mill, that they fully appreciated the extent of the abuse she had suffered. Many of the mill workers were initially reluctant to talk to them, but Geelan and Lawson badgered them until the workers agreed to share what they knew. The witnesses' initial reticence actually made them more valuable as witnesses. Since they were not intent on helping Judy, their testimony on her behalf was much more credible.

Geelan also requested all of the prosecutor's files on Judy's case, many of which had not been disclosed before despite the state's obligation to provide them. While meticulously going over the chronology of the case, Geelan discovered that several statements and hearings had not been transcribed. He was particularly interested in the transcripts of Martha Henderson's taped conversations, since Martha's testimony during the trial simply did not ring true. The judge, in ruling on Geelan's motion, ordered the state to make the actual tapes available to him.

One of the most dramatic moments in Geelan's legal career came when he sat listening to the tapes in the office of Dennis Surrett, the state investigator. Geelan and Lawson tried to remain calm and poker-faced while they heard Martha Henderson say on the tape that Judy's initial reaction to news of the murder was shock. Her statement was consistent with Judy's insistence that she did not believe Jerry Henderson would kill her husband, but it was completely at odds with Martha's testimony at trial that Judy had knowingly hired Henderson to kill her husband. Martha's taped comment had never been disclosed before. Geelan and Lawson also heard Martha on tape before her conversation with Jerry Henderson. She warned the police officers who were strapping the recording devices on her, "Hey, don't touch that cocaine. I'm going to need it when I'm through with this call." When the tape was played for the jury, the prosecution conveniently started it after Martha's incriminating statement, which was also deleted from a transcript provided for the defense.

Many of the discrepancies Geelan discovered were not particularly significant in and of themselves, but they could have influenced the trial's outcome in their totality. For instance, Martha, who provided the most damning testimony against her sister at trial and who struck Geelan as the "biggest cheerleader for Judy's death," contradicted herself on several occasions that were neither noticed nor pursued. She testified at the trial that Judy was never scared or nervous after she arrived at Martha and Jerry's house in Georgia. However, on the undisclosed tape, Martha repeatedly described Judy as being scared that her husband would hurt her. These types of discrepancies favored Judy's claim that her reckless discussion with her sister and brother-in-law was motivated by fear. They also could have offset the prosecution's portrayal of Judy as a liar who could not be trusted. Indeed, the assistant district attorney arguing the case told the jury that Judy was making up the abuse she had allegedly suffered, pointing to all of her other "lies" as evidence of her lack of credibility.

"If I rang a bell for every time this woman lied," he told the jury, "we'd all be deaf."

. . . .

At the pretrial conference preceding the evidentiary hearing on Judy's state habeas petition, Geelan informed Judge Fielding that he would need at least seven days to present his case. The state argued that such hearings never last more than two days. Judge Fielding set aside three days in February 1997, assuring Geelan that additional days could be added at a later time in the unlikely event they would be necessary.

Geelan and Lawson had lined up twenty-three witnesses to testify on Judy's behalf. The first witness was called at 1:00 P.M. on the first day of the hearing, but the state immediately objected to her testimony, declaring that it was impermissible hearsay. Lawson, who was examining the witness at the time, argued that the Alabama statute governing sentencing hearings, when the testimony in question should have been elicited in the first place, expressly provided for hearsay testimony. The state maintained that the statutory provision allowing for as much information as possible to be heard at a sentencing hearing was only intended to benefit the prosecution. Judge Fielding, reluctant to simply credit either side's interpretation of the statute, told the Kaye, Scholer team that they could have fifteen minutes and the use of the courthouse law library upstairs to locate a case on point.

While Lawson and John Howley, the most senior member of Geelan's team, frantically looked for relevant case law in the judge's library, Geelan rushed down the street to a phone in a nearby law office and called the Southern Center for Human Rights. He frantically told the receptionist that he needed to speak with Bright about an urgent matter, and explained the situation to Bright as soon as he picked up the phone. Bright began what Geelan remembers as an erudite and detailed discussion of the relevant case law.

"I don't have time for this!" Geelan yelled into the phone. "I need something *now*!"

Bright then put another attorney on the line who had recently argued a similar issue, and he was able to quickly pull up his brief on his computer and give Geelan some helpful citations.

Unfortunately, Judge Fielding ruled that none of the cases was exactly on point because none involved a state habeas hearing. He therefore sustained the state's objection, but he did so in such a way that much of the objectionable testimony was nonetheless elicited. Judge Fielding deemed much of the hearsay testimony acceptable on a case-by-case basis as long as Geelan and Lawson established that Judy had discussed her abuse with the witness close to the time in which it had happened.

The first day's witnesses consisted exclusively of Judy's former coworkers at the mill. Most of them had long since lost touch with her, rendering their testimony about the abuse they had observed and heard about practically unimpeachable in its honesty and objectivity. It eventually became clear that it was pointless to cross-examine them, and the state essentially ceased doing so. Their testimony was extremely powerful in its simplicity and repetitiveness. Judy's former coworkers all essentially testified to the fact that Judy was in a constant state of fear and was continuously beaten for the duration of her marriage. Many stated that they had noticed Judy with severe bruises and black eyes for years. Several testified that Judy was petrified of her husband, and that "when he got mad he went crazy and just went on a rampage." They also recalled that he had repeatedly threatened to kill Judy and the children or take the children away from her if she ever left him.

On the second day of the hearing, Lawson conducted a direct examination of Gary Haney, Judy's son. He was twenty-three at the time of the hearing, but his testimony focused on his recollection of his childhood up until he was nine years old. Judge Fielding had interrupted Gary early in his testimony to ensure that the abuse Gary was referring to was "something different from a spanking or something." As soon as Gary provided examples of the abuse he and Tonya had suffered at the hands of their father, it became clear that their experiences went far beyond acceptable limits of corporal punishment.

Gary recalled the time when he was chased by a pit bull at age six or seven and jumped in the back of his father's truck to protect himself. The pit bull jumped in after him, scratching the side of the truck. "He hit me good for that," Gary testified. "He whipped me with a belt and tossed me across the kitchen floor." Then there was the time Gary and Tonya were cleaning honeysuckles off the fence at their father's behest, and he heard them complaining about how hot it was outside. "He gave us both a whipping with a cane pole type object," Gary recalled. "Then Tonya was showing me her whelps on her legs, and he seen her doing that, and he gave her another whipping for her showing me the whelps on her legs." Another time Gary was beaten on the legs and buttocks with a leather belt because it took him ten minutes to retrieve the gloves his father had left out in the pasture.

Gary also testified about the verbal abuse his father doled out, such as screaming and yelling at Gary for striking out when he played baseball. "There was some days he made me feel like a son," Gary said, "and then there was some days he made me feel like a nobody."

Gary described as well the more intensive abuse his father inflicted on his mother, such as choking her with a broom or beating her with a poker. He also recalled several instances when his mother had to hide from his father or lock herself in a room to protect herself from his wrath. Gary provided other chilling vignettes of what it was like to live with his father:

> I remember one morning. We was eating breakfast, and my dad went to get a sausage biscuit out of the biscuits that my mom made. The biscuits crumbled up, and he took a glass of orange juice and dashed it in my mom's face, and he was yelling at her and screaming at her and putting her down, saying, "You should know how to make biscuits! I can't believe you don't know how to make biscuits!" And my mom pleaded with him, and she said, you know, "I'll make you some more biscuits." He kept screaming and hollering, and my mom was at the stove making more biscuits, and he'd argue back at her. He walked up to her and kicked her in the butt. . . . He was wearing leather cowboy boots with pointed toes."

Judy's brother-in-law Billy Haney, who had been cordial but distant to Geelan and his colleagues during the time leading up to the hearing, seemed to soften toward them as the testimony developed. When the prosecutor got up to cross-examine Gary after his two hours of testimony on direct examination, Billy motioned for him to sit back down. During the recess, Billy took his nephew out to lunch. It was obvious to even the most casual observer that Billy was touched by Gary's heartfelt account of what it had been like living with Billy's big brother.

On the third day of the hearing, the state presented Geelan with two handwritten lists entitled "State v. Haney—Discovery." Geelan had already been given two lists as part of pretrial discovery, but these lists were different. One was an unsigned and undated list of evidence that had been provided to the defense, and the other was a shorter list that appeared to be a subset of the first list. It was immediately clear to Geelan that several things were missing from both lists, such as the incriminating statements made by Martha Henderson. Geelan noted that, according to the lists, neither of the tapes in question had been provided to the defense. The state insisted that the tapes had been produced, and that the lists in question were simply preliminary, incomplete lists of the discovery provided.

At the state's insistence that other lists did, in fact, exist, Judge Fielding called a recess and granted the state some time to find the additional lists. This gesture followed the state's outburst at Geelan, who had pondered aloud why it was that there seemed to be a pattern of assuring him that the state had given him every possible piece of evidence, only to find that more could always be produced when he made additional motions to solicit it.

The state returned from the recess with two additional discovery lists. Any suspicions Geelan may have had about the lists being fabricated were dispelled once he saw that they were written in faded pencil and had frayed pages. They were undisputably genuine, but they, too, were incomplete. Once again, they failed to mention either of the Martha Henderson tapes in question.

John Howley was responsible for questioning Dennis Surrett (the state investigator) about the missing tapes and other *Brady* issues. With Surrett on the stand, Howley methodically worked his way through every list the state had provided.

"Do you see Martha Henderson's name on *that* list?" he'd ask.

"No, I do not," Surrett would reluctantly reply.

Once he got Surrett to agree that Martha was not on a particular list, Howley moved on to the next one. As he did so, Geelan noticed that the prosecutors became increasingly quiet. He knew that his chances of prevailing on a *Brady* claim remained remote, since he would have to show not only that the state failed to turn over evidence, but also that its failure to do so had an impact on the outcome of the case. He doubted such an argument would convince Judge Fielding, who had, after all, presided over the initial trial. Judge Fielding was an elected official, however, and he had been criticized in the local papers for doing whatever District Attorney Rumsey asked him to do. Geelan also knew that the state was no longer quite so confident in its dismissal of Judy's claims. By the end of the third day, it was clear to everyone that Geelan's original request for a seven-day hearing had not been outlandish, and that he would still have plenty of arsenal at his disposal when the case resumed.

Even though Geelan's "big guns" had not testified yet, including the psychiatrist who could diagnose Judy as a battered woman and the doctor who could corroborate the fact that her trial counsel had been drunk, he figured the threat of their testimony was as powerful as their actual testimony would be. He knew that there would be no better time to try to settle the case than at the conclusion of the first three days of testimony.

. . . .

Bright and Norby, who had served as Geelan's mentors and advisors throughout his handling of the case, had informed him that it was highly unlikely that the attorney general's office would agree to settle the case for a sentence that was less than death unless the victim's family was onboard. In Judy's case, Billy Haney would have to agree to leniency for the woman who had been found guilty of murdering his brother. This was, after all, the man who had found his older brother with his face blown off and gunshot wounds to his stomach. Would he even consider some kind of a deal?

Kelly Lawson called Billy after the hearing and asked him if she and Geelan could talk to him. He agreed to meet them for dinner. The meal was emotional and long, lasting over three hours, but Geelan and Lawson left it feeling that they had made definite progress. Even though Billy maintained that he trusted the attorney general's office to do the right thing, he also admitted that the prosecutors had disclosed to him that there were problems with their case. He agreed with Geelan and Lawson that no one would be served by having to go through the entire trial again, not to mention the additional suffering Gary and Tonya would endure if their mother was executed. He promised to think about what they had proposed. While the ideal outcome would have been for Billy to offer his total support for his sister-in-law, Geelan considered it a victory that Billy was willing to listen and did not insist on Judy's execution. There was hope.

Geelan wrote to Billy as soon as he returned to New York and called him one month later. Billy continued to be noncommittal, but promised he'd think about it some more.

"Let's see what happens with the case," Billy told Geelan.

When Geelan, Lawson, Gary, and Billy dined together a second time, it was clear that Billy was edging closer to agreeing to a settlement. By the end of the meal, he told Geelan and Lawson he would not oppose a decision by the state to reduce Judy's death sentence.

· · · · · · · ·

Geelan had grown extremely fond of Judy and was not convinced that she deserved to be incarcerated at all. He found himself wondering what would happen if he were able to get a new trial for Judy. Bright and Ruth Friedman, a seasoned Southern Center for Human Rights attorney who worked in Washington, D.C., set him straight.

"Are you nuts?" Friedman cried. "If you can settle for life, do it. That's a victory. That's what you fight for in a death penalty case."

"How are you going to feel two years from now when Judy is in the electric chair and you had the opportunity to settle?" Bright asked.

Geelan found it hard to believe that any state would actually carry through with an execution of a woman who had an abusive husband and a drunk attorney. But he was out of his element, and he knew it.

"I have to defer to the experts," he concluded to himself. "I'm a civil litigator. I work with corporations." This was, after all, Talladega, Alabama, where the death penalty was routinely imposed in cases that people elsewhere would never consider worthy of death.

Geelan called Clay Crenshaw, a prosecutor with the attorney general's death penalty unit. He sensed that Billy would go along with a settlement if the state cooperated.

"Any interest in settling this?" he asked Crenshaw.

Crenshaw agreed to meet with Geelan, but informed him that any deal would have to be approved by the local district attorney who had initially tried the case. Geelan laid out the problems with the case before Crenshaw.

"I started this case with a drunk attorney and some missing medical records," he said. "But I think you'll agree that I'm now a hundred miles past that."

Crenshaw was dismissive of Geelan's *Brady* claims, but he acknowledged that Geelan had a strong ineffective assistance of counsel claim regarding the lack of mitigating evidence presented at sentencing. Crenshaw also pointed out, however, that it was not his call to make.

"This case is not going to settle," he told Geelan, "if Billy Haney and the local D.A. [district attorney] don't want it to."

"If you guys agree, he'll agree," Geelan assured him.

At Geelan's urging, Crenshaw set up a meeting in Talladega County with the local district attorney and Billy Haney. After the meeting, Crenshaw called Geelan and told him they were willing to settle.

"We'll give her life without the possibility of parole," he said.

Geelan knew any settlement offer was a victory, but it was hard to feel elated. The executions of women in Texas and Florida in 1998 have since provided him with closure on his nagging doubts about whether he did the right thing. He now knows that his confidence in Alabama's reluctance to execute a woman was misplaced.

What most comforted Geelan, however, and allowed him to accept the reduced sentence the state offered was his client. After he explained everything to Judy, she summed up the situation in her characteristically direct way.

"Life beats the hell out of death," she said.

. . . .

While Judy is relieved and grateful to have escaped death, she has struggled to adjust to her new home. In describing her life at Tutwiler Women's Prison, she writes:

> *The prison life is not what I thought it would be. The inmates have it much harder then I thought. Everything is hurry up and then wait. They rush us to eat our meals then we stand in line five or ten minutes. It is the same way when we go to pill line. We have to stand in pill line for our medication 30 minutes to one hour sometimes more it all depends on who is running the pill line. We only get five to seven minutes to eat our meals, sometimes the officers don't give us that much. The food is half cook, most of the time it has no taste whatsoever. We get no fruit or milk. We are all so lacking in vitamins till it's not funny any more. We are having trouble with leg cramps and it is overcrowded till you can't breath, and so hot in the summer time. We have 3 big fans in*

our dorm with 140 women. Our dorm is almost as long as a football field with no ventilation whatsoever then the windows. There is always fight brecking out over who gets the fan to blow over them, and then we have to deal with the mates, or if you will, husbands and wifes. They are always fighting each other and anybody else who specks to there mates.

By far the most difficult aspect of Judy's incarceration, however, is being separated from her two children. In a letter to Norby after her sentence was reduced, Judy wrote, "Tonya and Gary are thrill two, that death sentence wasn't helping them much either." When Judy was first locked up in 1984, her children were separated not only from her, but from each other as well. Tonya moved in with Judy's sister Betty so that she could continue going to the same school. She has settled down not far from where she grew up and has two children of her own. Gary lived with Judy's sister Linda McKeen until he was sixteen and then moved in with Jerry's parents. He and Tonya both write to Judy regularly, and visit her on holidays.

Judy's first two years on Death Row were the most dismal. She was filled with hatred for everyone, and felt bitter and vindictive about the way she had been treated by her attorneys, her family, and the judicial system. The prison chaplains, who met with her regularly, were ultimately able to convince her that she was hurting only herself by holding onto her hatred; it was time to move on. Judy found it particularly difficult to truly forgive Martha, who she felt betrayed her the most. But with her forgiveness and acceptance of her current lot in life has come an emotional release that has helped Judy retrieve her sense of humor and positive outlook.

"God's going to work something out for me," she says. "We're all going to die someday anyway. It's in His hands, so I'm just not going to worry about it."

Everyone who encounters Judy is impressed by her large size and her engaging sense of humor.

"She's funny as all get out," Norby recalls. "And very motherly. She was always trying to take care of me."

Marion Thornton, the warden's secretary at Tutwiler, is particularly fond of Judy because they are both from Talladega County. She still chuckles over the note Judy wrote her requesting a brassiere to wear during her state habeas hearing. "You and I both know those folks in Talladega County ain't never seen a 48 triple D bosom before," Judy wrote.

Even discussions of the abuse she suffered could be tinged with humor.

When Geelan was trying to pin down the exact date of her mother's funeral because the hospital records for the broken nose she had sustained at the time were missing, Judy insisted the year was 1977.

"I lost Elvis in August of '77 and Mama in September of '77," she said. "John, it was a double blow."

The positive regard Geelan has for Judy is certainly reciprocated. In reflecting on her case, Judy wrote:

> *To me my first trial was a big joke. I was not perpare or my children either. They call no witness to help prove my abuse or anything else. As you know Mr. Blair was found drunk and lock up for 24 hours after that he didn't open his mouth. When I got Charlotta Norby she was good. She done all she could for me, but things really started to change for me when I got John Geelan and his law firm, they had the money to back them and do a real in depth investigation. I will always be in John Geelan's debt for all he has done for me. He has been a really good friend and lawyer. He has help me buy my medication and even bought me a fan to use on death row when I didn't have money on my books to pay for it myself.*

Judy is not a particularly religious woman, but she believes that God works miracles. She is convinced that God sent her Geelan, and that He will also find a way for her to walk out of prison.

"You've got to have faith," Judy says, "Because a person without hope is no person at all."

jimmy lee horton

Replaying the scene in her mind over the years, Ayoka wished she could stop at the moment when Jimmy Lee came into her room. Initially, she simply wanted to stop time so that she could figure out what to do to change what happened next. Surely there must have been something she could have said or done, had she not been so sleepy, to make things turn out differently. Later, when Ayoka accepted the fact that Jimmy Lee's arrest and conviction were beyond her control, she still wanted to hit the Pause button as he entered her room. She had been happy then.

Ever since Jimmy Lee had moved in with Ayoka and her mom, he was the one who would watch her while her mom worked the night shift. That night, though, he had said he had something to do, so he arranged for Billie, the girl from across the street, to babysit her. Ayoka tried to wait up for him, but she finally gave up and went to sleep. She vaguely remembers his coming home and then walking Billie back across the street. What really woke her was the racket her two dogs made when Jimmy Lee walked back in the house.

"Shush up!" she heard him say. "What's gotten into you two?"

There were also bizarre bursts of flashing lights and scuffling sounds, which she later realized must have been the police surrounding the house. Then the phone rang two times, and each time Jimmy Lee seemed to do a lot of listening and very little talking.

After the second phone call, Jimmy Lee came into her room and sat on her bed to wake her, although she was far from asleep at that point. He was clearly agitated.

"I gotta go," he said.

Even at nine years old, Ayoka could tell he was scared.

"You just stay in bed, okay?"

It was impossible to get back to sleep. Ayoka heard Jimmy Lee leave through the front door, followed by a big thump and some shouting. She pulled the covers around herself and lay very still, trying desperately to figure out what was going on. The struggle that Jimmy Lee was involved in just outside the house was then brought into the house, along with a lot of voices Ayoka had never heard before.

One of the voices came up the stairs and into her room. It belonged to a man with a sheriff's hat and badge.

"I'm Officer Gant," he said, looking very big and imposing from Ayoka's vantage point in bed. "Your daddy asked me to come get you."

Ayoka cautiously followed the officer downstairs and saw a bunch of men surrounding Jimmy Lee, who was sitting in a chair with his back to her. As she got closer, Ayoka noticed with alarm that his hands were handcuffed around the back of the chair. It didn't look very comfortable.

The officer led her around to the front and, at Jimmy Lee's request, lifted her onto his lap. Ayoka put her arms around him and snuggled into him. He couldn't hug her back, but she could tell he wanted to. She rested her head on his chest and listened to his heart thump. The thumping grew faster and louder as one of the men read Jimmy Lee something about his rights.

. . . .

Jimmy Lee Horton was born on November 25, 1952, in Macon, Georgia. He was the eleventh of twelve children, and had four sisters and seven brothers. His parents did the best they could to care for their large brood. Jimmy Lee's father built caskets for a funeral home, and his mother brought in extra income by doing some babysitting. Even though the children were always fed and clothed, Jimmy Lee remembers feeling poor. He didn't have things other kids had, even kids in his own low-income, black neighborhood, and he resented it.

Coveting things his parents simply could not buy, Jimmy Lee began to steal them. At first, he and his friends would steal bicycles and take them for joyrides, but he soon progressed to shoplifting and robbery. By the time Jimmy Lee was fifteen, he was getting arrested on a regular basis. Law enforcement officials frequently visited his house, carting him off on at least three occasions to juvenile facilities. He was always released to his parents' custody with admonitions to clean up his act.

His parents were bewildered by their son's delinquency (their other children had no trouble with the law) and imposed rules that Jimmy Lee would either break or get around. In an attempt to straighten out Jimmy Lee and improve his failing grades, his mother insisted that he not leave the house until all of his homework was completed. But Jimmy Lee convinced his brother Larry, one year older and a far better student, to do his homework for him.

In the summer of 1971, Jimmy Lee was arrested for burglarizing a store in Macon. He had committed several burglaries in the past, but this was the first time that he was caught. Since he was nineteen at the time of the burglary, Jimmy Lee did not go to a juvenile facility this time. He was sentenced instead to twelve years at Arrendale (Lee) Correctional Institute in Alto, Georgia, a long way from his hometown of Macon.

Prison was scary. The older prisoners were constantly picking on the younger inmates, often taking advantage of them sexually or taking their food and possessions. Another hardship was that Jimmy Lee was separated from his girlfriend, Delores Chambers, who was pregnant with Jimmy Lee's child. On December 6, 1971, six months after Jimmy Lee entered prison, his son, Rodney Chambers, was born. On Valentine's Day, 1975, one month after his release (as a result of credit for time served and an early discharge), Jimmy Lee married Delores.

After a short stint of living with his parents, Jimmy Lee was able to find a place for his family to live. He found work at the Weaver Vault Company, building caskets like his father. The owner gave Jimmy Lee a break since he liked his father. After two years, however, he had to cut back on staff and he let Jimmy Lee go. Three months later, Jimmy Lee found work as a janitor at a local elementary school. He also made extra money working for Ray Willis, the sheriff of Bibb County, who had a side business doing residential painting.

For a while, Jimmy Lee enjoyed his quiet family life. He was able to save some money, since his rent was very cheap and his expenses were low. He was no longer in touch with his old buddies because he had no desire to return to his old habits. He preferred staying home and playing with his son. By 1977, however, just two years into the marriage, Jimmy Lee was bored. He began going to clubs, where he fooled around with other women and hooked up again with his old buddies. He and Delores began to fight regularly.

One night, Jimmy Lee ended up at a club called Flaming Sally, where he ran into a former girlfriend. Clemenstine Collins, more than ten years his senior and the mother of a young daughter, soon became his girlfriend. Jimmy Lee had by then returned to other old ways as well. In the fall of 1977, he was caught burglarizing a tire store. He was given a six-year sentence, but would serve only half of that. For Delores, Jimmy Lee's estranged wife, it was the last straw. She filed for divorce in 1977, shortly after Jimmy Lee went to prison. Visiting him instead was Clemenstine, with whom he moved in after his release in 1980.

. . . .

Clemenstine stuck by Jimmy Lee while he was in prison, but she laid down the law when he got out. She made it clear that staying clean was a condition of living with her and her daughter, Ayoka. Jimmy Lee agreed and committed himself to finding work. Even though Clemenstine had a steady job at an egg crate factory, money was tight. Through a friend, Jimmy Lee found a part-time job as a carpenter, but he could work there only a couple days each week. At first he tried hard to find additional employment to cover the rest of the week. He also visited the unemployment office every day, where the officer knew him well. But when day after day produced no new job leads, Jimmy Lee ceased devoting his free time to finding work. He began instead to hang out with his friends, who were also unemployed.

On November 28, 1980, Jimmy Lee and four of his friends were hanging out at the Flaming Sally club, drinking beer and bemoaning their lack of jobs and money. Jimmy Lee needed little encouragement when Pless Brown, known as "Chug," suggested that he and Jimmy Lee go out and do something about getting themselves some money. Driving a blue pickup truck that they coowned with Hamp Davis (who stayed behind that night), they headed across town to a house that Brown knew was unoccupied at the time. They easily broke into the dark house and stole a black-barreled .22 caliber pistol and a television set. They took the hot property to Hamp Davis's house; Davis's wife agreed to sell the television to one of her coworkers at a local bank.

Jimmy Lee and Pless Brown continued to drive around town. They stopped at the Raintree Apartments, where one of the apartments was dark and apparently deserted. They broke into the apartment, which belonged to Sherrell Grant, and proceeded to commit their second burglary of the night.

In addition to taking some furniture, which they had loaded onto their truck parked in the back of the apartment complex, they also stole a silver-colored pistol. Now Jimmy Lee and Pless Brown both had a .22 caliber gun in their possession, the black-barreled one stolen earlier that evening and the silver pistol taken from Grant's apartment. Both guns would be fired that night, and it is still unclear who fired which gun. Jimmy Lee has always maintained that he started out with the silver gun, but that he switched guns with Brown later that night.

In the midst of the burglary, Jimmy Lee and Pless Brown saw approaching lights and realized they had been spotted. The two men hurried out the back door, thinking that they had plenty of time to make a clean getaway. As Jimmy Lee reached the corner of the back of the apartment building, a woman startled him by running after him and yelling, "Hey, you ain't going nowhere!" Jimmy Lee ran to the truck for cover and then turned and fired at the woman to scare her off. Even though Jimmy Lee always packed a gun for protection, as did every man he knew, he had never fired it at anything other than tin cans in his backyard.

More shots were fired, and then Brown ran to the truck. He jumped behind the wheel, and they took off into the dark streets.

Jimmy Lee asked Brown what had just happened back there.

"Well, we don't want to talk about it right now," Brown replied.

Nothing else was said as Jimmy Lee and Brown drove around. They finally pulled up in front of the Sundown Lounge. There, Brown told Jimmy Lee that the shots he had heard as he turned the corner toward the truck were in response to a man confronting Brown with a gun and saying, "I got you." Sherrell Grant's boyfriend, Don Thompson, had borrowed a neighbor's gun and pursued the burglars with it. He had failed to release its safety, however, so it did not go off when he fired it.

Jimmy Lee and Brown ordered beers, but Jimmy Lee's hands were shaking too hard to hold his beer. He called Clemenstine and told her to come pick him up at the Sundown Lounge. Once he was home, Jimmy Lee tried to calm himself down. His main concern was keeping Clemenstine from finding out what he had been up to because he was sure she would kick him out if she knew. He had given her his word that he had changed his ways.

The next morning, Clemenstine suggested they drive to Atlanta to do some Christmas shopping. At first Jimmy Lee declined, saying he wasn't in the mood. He then relented, thinking it would be good to get the hell out of Macon. At the start of their drive, the news came over the radio that Don Thompson, the county's district attorney, had been shot and killed in a bungled burglary at his girlfriend's apartment.

"Oh, shit," Jimmy Lee thought. "Shit, shit, shit."

He asked Clemenstine to take the wheel, telling her he was too sleepy to drive.

Returning to Macon at nightfall, Jimmy Lee was startled to see a blockade of police cars on Route 75. It was clear they were stopping and checking all trucks. A woman who lived in the apartment building where Thompson was shot had informed the police that she had seen a gun being fired from the passenger side of a blue Ford pickup truck in the parking lot. The truck had driven away before she could make out its occupants. Jimmy Lee was able to drive past the blockade unnoticed since he was driving Clemenstine's car.

That night, Jimmy Lee and Clemenstine had dinner at his mother's house. As they were leaving, Jimmy Lee's brother Larry approached him.

"You heard about your boy, didn't you?" he asked.

"What?" Jimmy Lee feigned ignorance, even though he was sure Larry had linked him with the blue Ford pickup truck the police were describing as the getaway vehicle.

"Dude got killed last night," Larry said, looking hard at Jimmy Lee.

"Man, I'm sorry to hear that," Jimmy Lee responded, and then yelled to Clemenstine that it was time to go.

Once home, Jimmy Lee's fears, which he had unsuccessfully tried to quell throughout the day, returned in full force. They were tinged with the awful additional knowledge that his and Brown's previous night's escapades now included murder.

"Whatsa matter, babe?" Clemenstine asked him. "You look like you seen a ghost or something."

"Nothin'," Jimmy Lee muttered, and then said it again in an attempt to convince himself as well as Clemenstine.

He went over to Hamp Davis's house to find out what he knew.

"Chug's already been by," Davis said when Jimmy Lee showed up.

"What did he tell you?" Jimmy Lee wanted to know.

"He said, 'We had to burn somebody last night.'"

In the ensuing days, the police were able to match the description of the truck to the one Hamp Davis was driving. They pulled Davis over on his way to go hunting and questioned him about the murder. Davis denied any knowledge of it and was able to provide the police with an alibi—his job at the local Air Force base—for the time of the burglary.

The police continued to question Davis, convinced that he was not telling them the full story. On December 11, 1980, they picked him up after work and questioned him for fourteen hours straight. They did not give him anything to eat until after midnight. Finally, Davis broke down and implicated both Jimmy Lee and Brown. Unbeknownst to Jimmy Lee, Davis also identified him as the triggerman. Since Davis had not been there, however, his version of the crime came from Brown.

· · · · · · · ·

Jimmy Lee returned home in the early morning of December 12 after a night of club-hopping while Clemenstine worked the night shift. He found the babysitter asleep on the couch and walked her back across the street to her home. When he returned to the house, he was surprised at the racket Ayoka's dogs were making. Then the phone rang.

"Can I speak to Jimmy Lee Horton?" a man's voice said.

"Yeah," Jimmy Lee replied. "That's me."

"You're being arrested for murder. You've got five minutes to come out of the house with your hands up."

Jimmy Lee hung up the phone and went over to the window. Police cars lined the street, lights flashing. All of his neighbors were on their front porches, their eyes fixed on his house. He went upstairs and woke up Ayoka and told her to stay in bed.

The phone rang again.

"If you don't come out with your hands up right now," the voice said, "We're going to come in and get you."

"I'm coming, I'm coming," Jimmy Lee assured him.

He opened the door and walked outside. The lights from the police cars were blinding, but he could see enough to make out a swarm of officers surrounding the house. He put his hands above his head and stepped off the sun porch. As soon as he did so, officers who had been stationed on the roof jumped down on top of him. They then led him back into the house and handcuffed him to a chair.

Jimmy Lee recognized one of the officers as Walter Gant, with whom he had gone to school. He asked Gant to go upstairs and get Ayoka. Other officers Jimmy Lee knew as a result of the work he had done for Sheriff Willis were also there.

The police read Jimmy Lee his rights. Before they took him down to the station, Gant and the other officers Jimmy Lee knew advised him not to say anything. "Just get up and walk," they said. "Don't say nothin' on the ride into town, either," they added.

Ayoka, who had cried and carried on when they separated her from Jimmy Lee, was taken to City Hall. Jimmy Lee asked Gant to call Clemenstine at work, but to be sure not to alarm her.

At the police station, Jimmy Lee's silence was no longer acceptable. Suddenly everyone wanted him to talk. They pressured him in a variety of ways, at first simply urging him to tell his side of the story.

"Brown already gave a statement," an officer named Garvey told him.

He then brought in a tape recorder and let Jimmy Lee listen to some of what Brown had said. He played the part where Brown fingered Jimmy Lee as the killer.

"You'd better talk to save your butt," Garvey said. "Otherwise it's all on you."

Jimmy Lee was furious and bewildered by Brown's betrayal. He didn't want to believe it, but he couldn't deny what he had heard. Still he said nothing.

Next they brought in Clemenstine, who was crying.

"Jimmy Lee, please tell them the truth. I don't believe you did this. Tell them. Just tell them."

Commander Bishop was put in charge of the investigation. He uncuffed Jimmy Lee and allowed Clemenstine to sit in his lap.

"Look, I'm tired," he said. "If you're not going to talk, we're going to have to lock you up."

Jimmy Lee agreed to answer their questions. His account of what happened was often rambling and contradictory, but he was adamant about his innocence. He readily admitted to the burglaries and to shooting at Sherrell Grant, but insisted he had not shot at Don Thompson.

He was then taken to the county jail and locked up.

. . . .

On that same day, a Saturday, Hugh Wallace came to see Jimmy Lee. He was a local attorney whom Clemenstine had called at Jimmy Lee's request. Jimmy Lee had often seen Wallace at the jail when he worked for Sheriff Willis. He figured anybody who had that many clients had to be pretty good.

Wallace was in his mid-fifties at the time, but he looked a lot older because of his heavy drinking. He was the kind of man whose signature included a smiley face. He was also the only attorney Jimmy Lee knew. Jimmy Lee gave him $1,600, which was everything he had, and Wallace agreed to take the case. He assured Jimmy Lee that he would get the court to appoint him to the case once the funds ran out.

The preliminary hearing was held the following day. It was the first time Jimmy Lee had seen Brown since being picked up, and he was unprepared for the fury that engulfed him. Cursing and yelling at him about betrayal,

Jimmy Lee lunged at his former friend. It took several officers to physically separate the two men.

The judge decreed that the two defendants would be tried separately. Jimmy Lee was to be tried first on February 27, 1980. While awaiting his trial in the county jail, he remained optimistic.

"I can beat this," he'd say to himself and others. "How can they find me guilty of something I didn't do?"

In the days following Jimmy Lee's arrest, a ballistics expert determined that Thompson was shot and killed with a copper-coated CCI bullet fired from the black-barreled pistol that had been stolen from the first house Jimmy Lee and Pless Brown burglarized. Jimmy Lee had hidden the gun in his house, but Clemenstine turned it over to the police. A search of the house, pursuant to a warrant, turned up Remington bullets similar to those fired at Sherrell Grant, but no copper-coated CCI bullets. A state crime lab weapons expert also noted that the gun in question contained only six shots, but witnesses reported hearing more than six shots fired the night of the killing.

. . . .

The circuit district attorney, Joseph W. Briley, was known by defense attorneys as "Death Row Joe." During his two-decade career as a prosecutor, he sought capital punishment over thirty times, more often than any other district attorney in the state. He was described in the local paper as "a tobacco-chewing country prosecutor, holding a cup for a spittoon in the courtroom." After he sought the death penalty four times despite repeated reversals by higher courts, it was noted that he "had a sense of what he could get away with in a courtroom and pushed it to the limits."

As the district attorney for the neighboring Ocmulgee Judicial Circuit, Briley expressed his strong interest in handling the prosecution of Jimmy Lee's and Pless Brown's cases to Charles Weston, who became acting district attorney for Bibb County upon district attorney Don Thompson's murder. Weston wished to avoid any appearance of a conflict of interest in handling the state's case against the two men accused of murdering his predecessor, and he agreed to let Briley serve as the lead prosecutor for both cases.

Briley sought the death penalty for both men, portraying each of them as the murderer. In his entire career as a prosecutor, Briley had been successful in convincing juries to oblige him with death sentences nineteen times. All but seven of those convictions, however, were reversed on appeal. Most of the reversals were a result of Briley's legendary use of peremptory strikes to keep blacks, women, and young adults off his juries.

Briley was unsuccessful in his efforts to create the jury that he was after in Pless Brown's case. Even though Briley used nine of his ten peremptory strikes to exclude blacks from the jury, in the end it consisted of five blacks and seven whites. Jimmy Lee was not so lucky. Using the same number of peremptory strikes that he had used in Brown's case, Briley was able to come up with a jury that was much more to his liking. There were no blacks on it.

. . . .

Jimmy Lee knew he didn't stand a chance as soon as the all-white jury was sworn in. He took the stand and testified that he had not shot at Don Thompson, but it made no difference. He believed he could have lined up one thousand upstanding citizens to testify for him, and they would not have swayed his jury. He was sure that all they saw was a poor black man accused of killing one of their own—a district attorney no less.

Briley made sure that the jury remembered the prominence of the victim. Even when claiming not to be focusing on the fact that Don Thompson was the county prosecutor, he did exactly that.

> **And ladies and gentlemen, let me make this clear at this point.**
> **Although I knew and admired Don Thompson as a fellow prosecutor, I'm not asking for the death penalty because Don Thompson was killed; not because the District Attorney was killed.**
> **What is so frightening, if he had been killed because he was the District Attorney, then that would not be something that concerned the average citizen.**

At trial, Jimmy Lee admitted to participating in the two burglaries and to shooting at Sherrell Grant, Thompson's girlfriend, but he claimed that Brown shot Thompson and later switched guns with him. Briley's case against Jimmy Lee was largely circumstantial. Grant testified that she had seen Jimmy Lee shoot at her with the black-barreled gun. That same gun, which had also been used to fire at and kill Thompson, was found in Jimmy Lee's apartment. The only direct evidence against Jimmy Lee came from

Hamp Davis, who testified that Jimmy Lee had told him that he had shot Thompson because Thompson had pulled a gun on him, and it was "either him or me." Davis also testified that Brown had told him that Jimmy Lee had shot Thompson.

In a rare show of effective lawyering on Jimmy Lee's behalf, Wallace was able to impeach Hamp Davis's credibility. He succeeding in showing the jury that Davis was initially a suspect in the shooting and had implicated Jimmy Lee only after being held and questioned for over fourteen hours. Wallace also pointed out that Davis's testimony could have been tainted by the fact that the district attorney's office was debating whether to prosecute his wife for selling the stolen television as well as participating in the sale of other hot items.

Jimmy Lee refuted Hamp Davis's account when he testified in his own defense. He also tried to undo the damaging evidence regarding the black-barreled gun, but his testimony was contradictory and confusing. He told the jury that he initially had the silver gun and that he later traded guns with Brown. But under cross-examination, Jimmy Lee changed his story several times. The only point he adamantly stuck to and insisted upon was that he did not have the black gun when Thompson was shot.

Briley did his own part to contribute to the jury's confusion about Brown's and Jimmy Lee's culpability, as evidenced by his often contradictory verbal maneuvering in his closing statement to the jury:

> And I want you to understand that by prosecuting Jimmy Horton, by asking for the death penalty, I'm not saying that he alone is to blame for the killing of Mr. Thompson. I do say that he fired the fatal shot. I don't say that Pless Brown is not equally guilty.
>
> Ladies and gentlemen, if a person was killed by two people beating him each with a ball bat, and it was determined medically that only one blow killed him, and you were unable to determine who held the bat, who hit him with the blow that killed him, would you conclude that just because you couldn't be absolutely certain beyond every doubt in the world which one did it that you ought to let both of them go free? Of course, you wouldn't. You would know that both of them were equally guilty. But for any of you, if any of you are having any trouble with the question of whether Horton held the gun that fired the fatal shot; if two people are firing at the same man and he dies and you don't

know which one of them held the gun that fired the fatal shot, then what difference does it make? They both intended to kill him. So there is really not a lot of difference.

The trial lasted for seven days. To no one's surprise, least of all Jimmy Lee's, the jury found him guilty of murder on February 26, 1981. They had deliberated for less than an hour. The following day, the jury was asked to decide on Jimmy Lee's sentence.

Briley had made it clear throughout the trial that the state was "requir[ing] and demand[ing] the death penalty in this case." Briley relied on Jimmy Lee's prior arrests and incarcerations for burglary and motor vehicle theft to portray Jimmy Lee as someone who had been given too many chances. Even though Georgia law prohibits any mention of parole to the jury, Briley alluded to it ominously and did his best to present the death penalty as the only option for Jimmy Lee:

The penitentiary is not punishment for him. He'll walk out when he gets ready. He'll be back on the streets committing more crime. He'll escape. He has—his career in crime is progressive. He has progressed to the point now that if the jury does sentence him to death, he has nothing to lose. He has nothing to lose. The only thing he's got left, the only manner in which this jury can punish him is by taking his life.

There was much to contest and rebut in Briley's argument, but Wallace failed to do so. Instead, he devoted almost the entirety of his closing argument to pleading for Jimmy Lee's life. He called no witnesses and offered no evidence in mitigation. He literally begged the jury for mercy, but did not give them any affirmative reasons to be merciful.

In fact, in several instances, Wallace seemed to be arguing against his client. He told the jury that Jimmy Lee was "not a very good person" or "a very important person." In praising Briley as "the best electric chair lawyer there is in the state of Georgia, and probably one of the better electric chair lawyers in the United States," Wallace admitted to the jury that "[t]he way he talked, it made me hate my client. But then, I try and descend, to get down from that sort of passionate thing, and try to be reasonable about the whole situation; and I don't hate him quite as much." He admitted to the jury that he found his task of explaining to them why Jimmy Lee should not die "virtually impossible."

In his half-hearted plea for Jimmy Lee's life, Wallace pointed out that his was "not a very big request" because he was asking "for the life of a worthless man, that's all." He concluded by saying, "Maybe Mr. Briley is right, maybe he's not. Maybe he ought to die; but I don't know."

The jury deliberated for just forty-five minutes and then sentenced Jimmy Lee Horton to death. Pless Brown was tried next, with Briley again serving as prosecutor. Even though Briley had fingered Jimmy Lee as the triggerman in his pursuit of the death penalty against him, he did not hesitate to identify Brown as the one who fired the fatal shots in Brown's case. Unlike Jimmy Lee's jury, however, Brown's jury included five blacks. Even though he was charged with and convicted of the same crimes as Jimmy Lee, he was sentenced to life in prison.

. . . .

Jimmy Lee's first emotion, upon hearing his sentence, was how much he had let down everyone who cared about him. His mother, who had recently had open heart surgery but had nonetheless made it to the courtroom every day, sat behind him crying. Clemenstine, who had taken him in and believed in him, was sobbing. Jimmy Lee felt numb and empty. He didn't know how a death sentence worked, and he wondered how much time he had left.

The deputies took him back to the county jail and Willis, who was still the sheriff, allowed Clemenstine to come see Jimmy Lee. She and Jimmy Lee cried and hugged each other, but she also let him know how disappointed she was in him.

"You promised you wouldn't get in no more trouble," she said. "You promised."

It soon became clear to Jimmy Lee that his sentence was not going to be carried out anytime soon. He remained incarcerated in the county jail until 1983, at which point he was transferred to Georgia's Death Row in Jackson.

Shortly after the trial, a fellow inmate by the name of Arthur Fryer got word to Jimmy Lee that he needed to talk to him and his lawyer. When both Jimmy Lee and Wallace were listening, Fryer told them that on the night of the murder, he had run into Pless Brown at the Sundown club after Jimmy Lee had left. Brown had confided to him that night that he had just killed a man.

Armed with an affidavit from Fryer, Wallace sought a new trial. At the evidentiary hearing, however, Fryer stated under cross-examination that he had shared this information with Jimmy Lee prior to the trial. Since this meant that the information was not, in fact, newly available, the court denied the request for a new trial.

In 1982, Jimmy Lee's conviction and sentence of death were affirmed by the Georgia Supreme Court. Wallace then informed Jimmy Lee that it was the end of the road for him. The court would pay him to represent Jimmy Lee only through his state appeals, so that was as far as he could go.

. . . .

In November 1982, Steve Bright attended a meeting of the Georgia chapter of the ACLU. The purpose of the meeting was to figure out what to do about all the Georgia Death Row inmates who needed lawyers. Like most such meetings, this one had an air of urgency because the Georgia legislature had recently enacted a new waiver provision. A number of the cases would have to be filed by the first of January in order to avoid waiving the defendants' right to appeal.

Since the right to counsel did not apply to postconviction proceedings, however, inmates were dependent on volunteer lawyers. To meet their needs, the Georgia Resource Center was later established; it monitors the state's capital cases and assigns attorneys to those who are unrepresented. But in the early 1980s, the process of matching Death Row defendants with attorneys willing to take on their cases was much more informal. The bulk of the work was handled singlehandedly by Patsy Morris, who was a volunteer at the ACLU. Morris stepped in once a case had been directly appealed in state court, since the local, court-appointed attorneys would no longer handle it at that point. She would call attorneys across the nation, begging them to take on these cases for which they would not be compensated, or even have their expenses covered.

By 1982, Morris had some assistance in this endeavor. The Southern Prisoners' Defense Commission, which Bright had recently joined, took on a large number of cases and also assisted in finding attorneys for some of the defendants who remained without counsel. The Georgia chapter of the ACLU took on some of the state appeals as well, assigning them to some of their cooperating attorneys. At the conclusion of the November meeting, however, when Bright and the ACLU had each taken the maximum number of cases they could handle, there remained a handful of cases that had not yet been assigned counsel. Bright agreed to try to find attorneys for the cases that were left, intending to reach out to some of his friends and former colleagues outside Georgia. One of the cases was Jimmy Lee Horton's.

. . . .

Andrew L. Lipps joined the Washington, D.C., firm of Whitman and Ransom in October 1982. It was a small firm of only six attorneys who specialized in white-collar criminal work; the job represented quite a change from the Washington Public Defender Service (PDS) Lipps had left to join the firm. He had been at Whitman and Ransom a little over two months when Bright phoned.

"Andy, I'm jammed," Bright said, after exchanging pleasantries. "I've got a series of death penalty cases here that need to be filed by January 1. Could you take one on?"

Lipps and Bright had been colleagues together at PDS before Bright left for Atlanta. It had not taken long for Bright to distinguish himself at PDS as one of the best trial attorneys around. Lipps recalls that when one of Bright's cases went to trial, the entire courtroom would be packed with colleagues from PDS as well as prosecutors eager to see Bright in action and perhaps learn something in the process. Lipps also admired Bright's tremendous dedication to the plight of his clients and the impoverished in general.

Lipps was eager to help. His only concern was that he had never handled a capital case before, but Bright assured him that he would assist him and serve as the local attorney. Bright told him about Jimmy Lee Horton, who had been big news in Georgia at the time of the crime but was not known nationally; Lipps agreed to take on Jimmy Lee's case.

Upon hanging up the phone, Lipps immediately approached Whitman and Ransom's managing partner and told him he wanted to take on a pro bono case for a defendant facing a death sentence in Georgia. He also told the managing partner that the case would require some immediate attention, since the state habeas petition (the appellate process that follows the state court proceedings) had to be filed by the first of the year.

Armed with his managing partner's blessing and the resources of the firm, Lipps devoted the next two weeks to researching and writing the state habeas petition. Lipps took over the case at the conclusion of the direct appeals through the state courts, which had culminated with the Georgia

Supreme Court's 1982 affirmation of Jimmy Lee's conviction and sentence of death. Ordinarily, prior to petitioning the Superior Court of Butts County in Jackson, Georgia, for state habeas relief, a defendant must first petition the U.S. Supreme Court for certiorari. Lipps did not do so, however, because there simply wasn't enough time. The Butts County Superior Court ultimately dismissed the habeas petition, which Lipps had managed to file by the January 1 deadline, as being premature. Contrary to the public's perception that attorneys handling capital cases delay the process as long as possible, Lipps was chastised for proceeding too quickly. He was undaunted and relieved that his client would no longer be perceived as having waived his right to appeal any further. Lipps waited until the U.S. Supreme Court denied the petition for certiorari and then refiled his habeas brief.

Early on, Bright and Lipps met on a Saturday to brainstorm about the legal issues they could raise on appeal. Having read the transcript of the trial, Lipps thought the case was rich with appellate issues. Bright, who was more experienced with the way such issues fared in the courts, was less optimistic. Both men agreed that Jimmy Lee's death sentence was the result of Briley's success in getting an all-white jury for Jimmy Lee. But Bright pointed out that such discrimination was exceedingly difficult to prove in court.

The standard for proving discrimination during jury selection was known as the *Swain* standard because it was established by the U.S. Supreme Court in the 1965 case of *Swain v. Alabama*; it was an impossibly high standard. In *Swain*, the Court made clear that prosecutors are presumed to be utilizing their peremptory challenges in order "to obtain a fair and partial jury." In order to rebut this presumption, a defendant must establish a prima facie (evident on its face) case showing that the peremptory challenges were exercised in a racially discriminatory manner. In other words, in order to prove discrimination under *Swain*, a defendant had to do more than show that the prosecutor struck all blacks in his case; he had to show that the prosecutor engaged in a practice of striking blacks from *all* cases. The court further articulated that a defendant could only do so by showing "the prosecutor's systematic use of peremptory challenges against [blacks] over a period of time."

The inherent challenge of such a standard stemmed not only from the difficulty of proving discrimination over a period of time, but from the expense and time needed to gather the necessary evidence to meet the court's standard for such discrimination. In locations where blacks represent 25 percent or more of the population, there is a great likelihood that even the most racially discriminatory prosecutor will nonetheless end up with blacks on his jury. In the 1986 decision *Batson v. Kentucky*, the U.S. Supreme Court agreed that *Swain* presented too high a standard, and overruled a significant portion of it. Jimmy Lee, however, had the misfortune of being governed by *Swain* rather than *Batson* because his conviction became final prior to the *Batson* decision.

Another claim that appeared promising to Lipps was ineffective assistance of counsel. Again, Bright did not share his optimism. Even though Bright agreed that Wallace's representation of Jimmy Lee had been atrocious, he had seen even more egregious lawyering pass muster with the courts. Such poor representation was typical because Georgia provided so little compensation for court-appointed lawyers.

As Bright saw it, the most promising issue to raise was that Hamp Davis's hearsay testimony about what Pless Brown had told him violated Jimmy Lee's constitutional right under the Sixth Amendment to confront his accuser. The law was murky, however, on the Confrontation Clause, so it was unclear whether Jimmy Lee could prevail on such a claim.

Bright and Lipps were able to identify several other issues that were intellectually sound, for which there was little or no supporting case law. There was no precedent, for example, for arguing that Briley's simultaneous pursuit of two men for the same crime constituted a violation of their right to a fair trial under the Fourteenth Amendment to the Constitution. Nor was there much case law to support the notion that Briley had overstepped his bounds by implying that Jimmy Lee should be sentenced more harshly because the decedent was a district attorney.

While the brainstorming session did not produce any clear winners in terms of issues to raise on appeal, it generated plenty for Lipps to work with. Sometimes the best case strategy is to raise only the issues that the attorney deems the most promising, so as to provide the client with the best shot without distracting the court and muddying the waters. In a capital case, however, one cannot afford to be selective. Any issue that can be raised and argued legitimately is worth pursuing because the risk of not doing so is too great. If any particular issue is not raised in the state habeas petition, the defendant loses the right to raise it later in federal court. Realizing that there was no chance the Georgia courts would grant relief on any issue, Bright and Lipps knew they had to preserve all of their claims for the federal courts to review. Even issues that do not have legal precedent at the time are worth pursuing, since the legal landscape can change significantly by the time the case actually reaches the U.S. Supreme Court. Lipps and Bright ended up raising over twenty-five legal issues in the state habeas petition they filed on Jimmy Lee's behalf.

The two attorneys strategized about which issues required an evidentiary hearing. Most of the claims made in the petition for Jimmy Lee could be argued and resolved by referring to the trial record and therefore did not require a hearing. The two claims requiring evidentiary hearings were the *Swain* claim and the ineffective assistance of counsel claim. Lipps and Bright argued the latter before the Butts County Superior Court. They decided that even if the court ruled against them (which it did), the record would still reflect how egregiously Wallace had handled Jimmy Lee's case.

The *Swain* claim, however, was a different matter. Lipps and Bright simply did not have the time or money to pursue it. Their request for funds to pay for an investigator to develop facts to prove the *Swain* claim had been denied by the Butts County Superior Court, and they were confident the court would rule against them on the claim's merits as well.

. . . .

State habeas proceedings are designed to allow the state court system to review and correct its own errors before the federal courts step in. As is often the case, however, the state courts that reviewed Jimmy Lee's case found no errors at all. Every single claim Lipps raised in his habeas brief was denied in the state habeas proceedings. The habeas petition was denied by the Superior Court of Butts County on November 7, 1986. The following year, both the Georgia Supreme Court and the U.S. Supreme Court refused to review the case.

On February 24, 1988, Lipps and Bright petitioned the U.S. District Court in Georgia for a writ of habeas corpus, contending that Jimmy Lee was convicted and sentenced to die in violation of the Constitution of the United States. Lipps was essentially raising the same claims he had in the state habeas petitions on Jimmy's behalf, and requested funds to pursue and present the *Swain* claim. Lipps argued that Briley had "engaged in a systematic practice of using peremptory challenges to strike blacks on [Jimmy Lee's] jury panel," and that he needed funds to pay for an investigation to develop the facts necessary to prove his claim.

The first victory for Jimmy Lee and his attorneys came on June 14, 1988. The district court agreed to fund an investigation of the *Swain* claim, decreeing that it could not rule on whether an evidentiary hearing on the matter was warranted until Lipps and Bright had been provided with a fair opportunity to prove the claim. The court concluded its order by urging counsel "to cooperatively arrive at the least expensive, most convenient, and most expeditious discovery procedures."

. . . .

Armed with their surprising victory, Lipps and Bright decided that it made more sense for Bright, as the local attorney, to oversee the investigation. Bright enlisted the help of Sara Whisennud, an investigator who later became a lawyer; Mary Brown Eastland, a paralegal; and several law student volunteers; they all devoted hundred of hours to documenting the proof they needed. Since they had to show a pattern of discrimination on Briley's part that went beyond Jimmy Lee's case, they compiled, charted, and analyzed the jury records for every one of Briley's cases that had gone to trial in the Ocmulgee Circuit since Briley had become district attorney in 1974. Briley's circuit consisted of eight counties (Baldwin, Greene, Hancock, Jasper, Jones, Morgan, Putnam, and Wilkinson), three of which did not save jury strike sheets. Bright and his staff were nonetheless left with a sufficient number of cases to prove their point. They analyzed a total of 25 capital cases and 159 non-capital cases that Briley had prosecuted.

In its attempt to reduce the obvious advantage enjoyed by the state, Georgia allows the defense counsel twenty peremptory jury strikes, compared with the ten afforded the prosecution. In each of the cases for which Whisennud and Eastland could obtain the jury records and the strike sheet, they recorded whom the defense had struck, whom the prosecution had struck, and the final composition of the jury. Since the jury records themselves did not reflect the race of the potential jurors, Whisennud and Eastland had to cross-reference the names they had charted with the voter registration lists for that year in order to document each person's race. The charts for Briley's capital cases involving black defendants and white victims were particularly compelling. Of the 103 strikes that Briley used in such cases, 96 were against black jurors, constituting more than 93 percent of his strikes.

Even though the charts seemed to prove unmistakable discrimination,

Bright and Lipps were taking no chances. Lipps knew a statistician, Dr. Gary Liberson, who agreed to help without pay. Liberson crunched the numbers and proved statistically that the racial bias Briley had employed could not be dismissed as coincidental.

The charts and statistical analysis that were critical to their *Swain* claim took Lipps and Bright more than a year to compile. Bright still did not think they had "a snowball's chance in hell" of winning on the issue, since no *Swain* claim had ever been sustained in Georgia. He had an additional piece of evidence in his arsenal to use against Briley, however.

· · · · · · · ·

Jimmy Lee, on Death Row in Jackson, Georgia, had grown increasingly pessimistic about his chances of getting his death sentence overturned. When he met Lipps in 1982, he was confident Lipps and Bright could do what Wallace had not been able or willing to do. It was immediately clear to Jimmy Lee that he now had attorneys who were zealously pursuing his case and his rights. In fact, it wasn't until Lipps and Bright took over his case that Jimmy Lee truly appreciated how poorly Wallace had represented him.

At their first meeting, Lipps confirmed Jimmy Lee's worst suspicions. "Wallace really screwed up," he said.

Jimmy Lee tried to be patient as he waited for Lipps and Bright to try to fix Wallace's mistakes. But as the years passed, he began to lose faith in the entire system. He tried to prepare himself for his inevitable execution.

He was not alone in his despair. Every Death Row inmate lives each day wondering how much longer he has to live. Each inmate deals with his impending death in his own way. Jimmy Lee preferred solitude and silence to the involved conversations he often saw others engaged in. A quiet and private person by nature, he had no desire to share his fears with anyone else. He was, however, willing to discuss his legal case with other inmates.

One day in 1988, during the time he was allowed to exercise in the yard, Jimmy Lee fell into conversation with a fellow inmate named Tony Amadeo. They began to discuss their cases and discovered that Steve Bright represented both of them. They also realized that Briley had prosecuted them both. Amadeo excitedly told Jimmy Lee that Bright had just won a significant victory in his own case in the U.S. Supreme Court by proving

Briley had directed jury commissioners to underrepresent blacks in jury pools.

For the first time in years, Jimmy Lee began to feel the stirrings of hope.

. . . .

The U.S. Supreme Court did indeed overturn Tony Amadeo's conviction of murder and his death sentence, finding that Briley had rigged the jury on the basis of race. Instrumental to Bright's victory in *Amadeo* was a memo he presented to the Court in which Briley directed jury commissioners to underrepresent blacks in the jury pools in a way that would elude detection and judicial scrutiny. (The memo was initially uncovered during an independent civil action involving a challenge to voting procedures in Putnam County.) The evidence was so compelling that Justice Byron R. White asked incredulously during argument, "There's never been any action against the prosecutor?"

The *Amadeo* memo was crucial to Jimmy Lee's case because it allowed Bright and Lipps to argue that Briley's intent could be inferred not only from the statistics they had compiled, but from his past discriminatory conduct as well.

They eagerly discussed how they could best make use of the *Amadeo* memo in Jimmy Lee's case. Together they formulated questions about the memo, which they would ask Briley at his deposition, scheduled for June 26, 1989. Lipps flew down to Atlanta to conduct the deposition, which took place in the state attorney general's office.

Unlike Bright, Lipps had never met the infamous prosecutor before. Briley, a large man with a deep voice, was clearly annoyed at having to be deposed at all. He had a confident, blustering manner and answered Lipps's questions curtly. At the outset, he announced that he had an appointment and could stay only two hours. The unspoken message he conveyed from the start was, "How dare you take up my time with such nonsense?" The fact that Lipps had flown down from Washington, D.C., solely to depose Briley did not impress him. Moreover, he adamantly refused to answer any questions about the *Amadeo* memo. The deposition ended without any answers from Briley about his role regarding the memo.

Lipps immediately filed a motion with Chief Judge Wilbur D. Owens Jr. of the U.S. District Court for the Middle District of Georgia to compel

Briley to both attend a second deposition and answer all of the questions asked of him. Judge Owens was the judge who had approved the funds for the *Swain* claim and would be ruling on the issue following the evidentiary hearing. Judge Owens wasted no time in firing off the order requested by Lipps, and he even had U.S. marshals serve it upon Briley.

The second deposition took place on July 14, 1989, in Gray, Georgia— Briley's home turf. Bright handled the questioning because Lipps was back in Washington, D.C. This time, Briley was compelled to answer Bright's questions about the memorandum he had written instructing the clerk of the court to underrepresent blacks in the jury pool. In response to Bright's questioning, Briley disclosed for the first time that he had written the memo in question, but he claimed he had done so at the direction of a judge, who was by then deceased.

During the evidentiary hearing that followed, Bright attacked Briley's version of how the memo came to be written:

> **The suggestion was made by Mr. Briley in his deposition and again here today that he really was trying to make it better. He says in his deposition, Your Honor, that he became aware that black people and women were underrepresented and he just went to Judge Jackson in chambers and said, "Judge, this isn't fair." And the judge said, "Well, I'm not going to let you put any more on than the minimum number." That's completely contradicted by the evidence we have. . . . The hearing was held in open court. Mr. Lawrence said Judge Jackson never gave Mr. Briley those kinds of instructions and, "I would remember if he did." We just heard Mr. Copeland say the same thing, that Judge Jackson never told Mr. Briley to put on the minimum number of women and the minimum number of black people to bring this up.**

Bright also cited other examples of Briley's intentional racial discrimination:

> **This Wallace case in Greene County tried back in 1979, where they started picking the jury in Greene County which, of course, has got an almost 50 percent black population. And once a few of the [black] jurors had been qualified, Mr. Briley went to the bench and said, "I agree now to the defense motion for a change of venue." The judge said, "Granted." The defense lawyer says, "Withdrawn." The judge says, "It is too late." And subsequently**

he moved the case over to Baldwin County. That is another one of these efforts. And of course once the case got to Baldwin County in the special plea of insanity trial, six strikes out of six against blacks.

Once Lipps and Bright established their prima facie case that Briley had exercised peremptory challenges so as to deny blacks "the right to participate in the administration of justice," Briley was given an opportunity to rebut the evidence. He could argue that his racially neutral selection procedures nonetheless produced historical and systematic disparity or that he had neutral reasons for striking blacks. As the U.S. Court of Appeals for the Eleventh Circuit later found, "protestations of innocence and blanket denials of bad faith intentions are inadequate."

In his defense, Briley argued that he did not base his peremptory strikes on the basis of race. Instead, he claimed he frequently sought and relied upon the advice of local sheriffs and sheriffs' deputies about venire (jury pool) members' reputations before striking any jurors. He would then strike them if they had a connection to the defendant, the defendant's family, or the defendant's attorney, or if they had a reputation for lawlessness. This was contradicted by the testimony of several sheriffs' deputies.

The evidentiary hearing on the *Swain* claim was held on October 18, 1989. At the hearing, Judge Owens denied Jimmy Lee's petition. He was the judge who had agreed to fund the research for the *Swain* claim, granted an evidentiary hearing, and compelled Briley's deposition. In the end, however, Judge Owens credited Briley's account of his race-neutral reasons for his peremptory strikes. Lipps and Bright promptly appealed the decision to the U.S. Court of Appeals for the Eleventh Circuit. They did not need to explain to their client that this appeal was the end of the road. There were no higher courts left to which to appeal other than the U.S. Supreme Court.

. . . .

When a case is appealed to the U.S. Court of Appeals, a panel of three judges is picked at random to review the case and render a decision. A rehearing *en banc*, "with the entire court," can then be requested, but it is rarely granted. Jimmy Lee's appeal was heard by Eleventh Circuit Judges Johnson, Birch, and Dubina; the latter two were Reagan appointees. The odds did not appear to be in Jimmy Lee's favor.

In early September 1991, Lipps was sitting in a conference room at his law firm discussing a patent case. Jimmy Lee's case, which he had been appealing for almost a decade, was far from his mind. He was interrupted by his secretary, who informed him that a Stephen Bright was on the phone.

"I told him you were busy," she apologized, "but he said it was important."

"Andy," Bright said excitedly when Lipps picked up the phone. "I knew you'd want to be interrupted with this. We just got a decision in Jimmy Lee Horton's case." He paused to catch his breath. "We won!"

On September 3, 1991, the U.S. Court of Appeals for the Eleventh Circuit reversed the district court's denial of Jimmy Lee's writ of habeas corpus and remanded the case to the district court with instructions to grant the writ, conditioned on the state's right to retry the petitioner within a reasonable time. Bright and Lipps, who would have been thrilled with prevailing on one of the claims they had raised, had convinced the court on three of them.

Judge Frank Johnson's unanimous opinion held that (1) Briley's exercise of his peremptory strikes against black venire members was unconstitutional; (2) Wallace's poor closing argument and his failure to present mitigating evidence at Jimmy Lee's sentencing resulted in ineffective assistance of counsel; (3) the admission of Pless Brown's hearsay statements violated Jimmy Lee's constitutional right to confront witnesses, even though coconspirator's hearsay statements are admissible under Georgia law.

Despite the fact that the opinion was unanimous, both Lipps and Bright credit Judge Johnson with saving Jimmy Lee's life. Johnson was the senior judge of the three on the panel, having been on the bench for more than thirty years. It was his persuasiveness that resulted in a unanimous opinion.

Turning first to the *Swain* claim, the court expressed great satisfaction with the considerable evidence Lipps and Bright gathered about Briley's prosecutorial conduct in order to demonstrate a prima facie case against Briley. In discussing the infamous memorandum in which Briley outlined his plan to underrepresent blacks, women, and individuals between the ages of eighteen and twenty-four on Putnam County's grand and traverse (trial) juries, the court declined to make a factual finding on whether Judge Jackson actually ordered Briley to write the memo. The court made clear in a footnote, however, that it found Briley's claim to that effect to be entirely incredible. The court pointed out that even if Judge Jackson had

ordered Briley to write the memo and engage in the unconstitutional behavior advocated in it, Briley's responsibility as an officer of the court was
to note his objections on the record and refuse to engage in the subsequent
cover-up, neither of which he did.

The court also found Dr. Liberson, the statistician Lipps had secured,
to be more credible than Dr. Katz, the state's statistician. Dr. Katz basically
tried to show that Briley did not utilize many opportunities to strike blacks.
Dr. Liberson concluded that in the three counties for which full statistical
analysis was possible, the likelihood that Briley used a race-neutral method
for exercising the strikes was less than 1 in 100,000.

After finding that Bright and Lipps had made a prima facie showing of
intentional and systematic prejudicial behavior on Briley's part, the Eleventh Circuit Court of Appeals rejected the state's attempt to rebut Liberson's statistical conclusions about Briley by claiming that Briley had employed "racially neutral selection procedures" that unfortunately had a
disparate impact on black venire members. The court also rejected Briley's
claims that he had relied on sheriffs and deputy sheriffs for advice about
whom to strike. The officers in question either denied having advised Briley on many of the cases he specified, or agreed that they had advised
him, but not in the manner he claimed. Deputy Sheriff Columbus Johnson
described at least two of the venire members, whom he allegedly had told
Briley to strike from one of the juries, as "pillars of the community."

The court did not credit Briley's claim that he struck black venire members because they may have known the defendant or the defendant's family
or lawyer, since his strike pattern did not change in the six trials in which
venue was changed. The court noted in summation, "We have no choice
but to conclude that Mr. Briley's proffered reason was pretextual."

Lipps and Bright overcame equally large obstacles in order to prevail on
their ineffective assistance of counsel claim. The standard, established in
1984 in the case of *Strickland v. Washington*, is a two-pronged test that
requires a defendant to establish that his trial counsel's performance was
deficient, and, in addition, that this deficient performance prejudiced the
defendant.

The performance prong of the *Strickland* test is a particularly high
hurdle because the U.S. Supreme Court held that courts should presume a
counsel's effectiveness and consider all of the circumstances when assessing
the reasonableness of particular decisions. This presumption, coupled with
the Court's caution against second-guessing with the benefit of hindsight,

cloaks many poor performances by trial counsel in a protective and often impenetrable shield.

In their appellate brief, Lipps and Bright mentioned many instances of Wallace's ineffectiveness. During the state evidentiary hearing, Wallace had attempted to justify his conduct as the product of a "tactical decision." Such wording was clearly designed to hide behind the U.S. Supreme Court allusion, in *Strickland*, to an attorney's "strategic decisions," which, the Court said, deserved deference. Indeed, the Superior Court of Butts County had accepted Wallace's justifications as strategies and tactical decisions, and had ruled that Jimmy Lee had not been denied competent counsel.

In support of their claim that Wallace's failure to present mitigating evidence at Jimmy Lee's sentencing constituted deficient representation, Lipps and Bright gathered the affidavits of ten individuals who claimed they would have testified on Jimmy Lee's behalf at his trial had they been asked to do so. (Many of them did testify at the state habeas hearing.) Such testimony at the trial would have allowed the jury to see Jimmy Lee as a hard worker, a good youth, and someone who was able to provide for his common-law wife and their daughter. The jury would also have learned that Jimmy Lee had successfully adjusted to previous stays in prison and was therefore not an escape risk.

There was no good reason why any defense attorney would not want to present such powerful testimony. Wallace tried to excuse his poor performance with an explanation that defied reason. He stated that he had not gathered or presented such testimony because mitigating evidence was appropriate, he felt, only in gruesome cases involving torture. As he explained it, he believed that the jury would somehow conclude that "it was a horrible [torture-filled] case when it wasn't." The Butts County Superior Court had no problem accepting this explanation, ruling that it was a reasonable tactical decision on his part.

The Eleventh Circuit Court of Appeals had a different view, finding that Wallace had completely misunderstood the purpose of presenting mitigating evidence and had failed even to investigate the evidence that was available. The court took issue with Wallace's explanation as well:

> **Moreover, Horton's trial attorneys' [Wallace's and the other court-appointed attorney's] explanation that they thought that a discussion of mitigating circumstances would somehow imply that the case was torture-filled when it was not is unacceptable.**

**A jury who has already heard the evidence during the guilt
phase, including the coroner's report, obviously would know if
the case involved torture. It is unreasonable to assume that a jury
would somehow infer from the fact that the defense presented
mitigating evidence that the defendant engaged in torture.**

The court also found that Wallace's performance during the sentencing
phase of Jimmy Lee's trial was unreasonable because he attacked his client's
character. The court noted that comments such as "I ask you for the life of
a worthless man" and "[m]aybe he ought to die, but I don't know" virtually
encouraged the jury to impose the death penalty. Moreover, the court
noted, Wallace attempted to separate himself from Jimmy Lee during closing argument.

**Mr. Wallace explained that he and his co-counsel were appointed
counsel; that they were local lawyers and not "bleeding heart,
anti–death penalty lawyers"; that the reason they were representing Horton was because it was their "civic duty"; and they stated
that they "have to deal with [the prosecutors] every day. It's important for me to stay in good with them. [I feel] there is a lot of
peer pressure on me [but] nobody has tried to pressure me."**

Having proven the performance prong of *Strickland*, Jimmy Lee next
had to establish prejudice from his counsel's unreasonable assistance in
order to prevail on the entire claim. In order to satisfy the prejudice prong,
a defendant "must show that there is a reasonable probability that, but for
counsel's unprofessional errors, the result of the proceeding would have
been different." In other words, a defendant cannot prevail under *Strickland*, even when he successfully proves the ineptitude of his trial counsel,
if his case was such that he would have been sentenced to death anyway.
In Jimmy Lee's case, most of the evidence against him was circumstantial,
and Wallace's errors had a direct impact on the outcome. Finding that
Jimmy Lee had met his burden of proof on the prejudice prong, the court
ruled that there was a reasonable probability that, but for Wallace's failure to present mitigating evidence and his unfortunate comments during
his closing statement, Jimmy Lee's trial could well have had a different
outcome.

Finally, the Court turned to Jimmy Lee's Confrontation Clause claim.
Lipps and Bright argued that Jimmy Lee's right to be confronted with the
witnesses against him was violated when Hamp Davis was permitted to
testify that Pless Brown told him Jimmy Lee was the triggerman. Davis's

statement amounted to hearsay, which is a statement made out of court, often by a person other than the witness testifying at trial. Hearsay evidence cannot be used because it denies a defendant the opportunity to confront the source of the statement. There are, however, several exceptions to the hearsay rule, such as statements that are made under circumstances that ensure their reliability. Under Georgia law, Brown's statement was admissible under the coconspirator exception to the hearsay rule because it was made while "[t]he culprits [were] still concealing their identity." The court agreed, however, that Brown's statements as related by Davis violated Jimmy Lee's right to confront his accuser. The court found that the hearsay in question was not reliable because

> **[t]he statement was exculpatory. Also, it was made days after the crime while the press was intently following the massive police investigation that was then underway. Finally, it was made to a friend while the declarant and the witness were drinking together in a bar. Simply put, this is not the sort of evidence that can properly form the basis of a conviction.**

Since the case against Jimmy Lee "was largely circumstantial and was fairly weak," the only evidence that he was the triggerman was his and Brown's alleged statements to Davis. The court therefore concluded that the error in admitting the unreliable hearsay in violation of the Confrontation Clause could not be viewed as harmless.

Having reversed the district court's denial of Jimmy Lee's habeas writ on the basis of these three separate claims, the court remanded Jimmy Lee's case to the district court "with instructions to grant the writ conditioned on the state's right to retry the petitioner within a reasonable time."

At this point the state of Georgia petitioned the U.S. Supreme Court for certiorari, but the Court refused to grant it. The state was consequently left with no choice but to retry Jimmy Lee Horton. To do so, it once again appointed Joe Briley as the prosecutor. Two decisions finding him to have acted unconstitutionally—in *Amadeo*, and in Jimmy Lee's case, when he refused to review the Eleventh Circuit's ruling—did not seem to have damaged his reputation as a district attorney.

After a year of legal wrangling, Briley agreed to accept a plea agreement in which Jimmy Lee was sentenced to life imprisonment. The plea agreement also stipulated that Jimmy Lee would not be eligible for parole until 2005, twelve years after the plea was entered.

. . . .

After several stints at different correctional facilities in Georgia, Jimmy Lee ended up at Wilcox State Prison in Abbeville, Georgia. The approximately 1,100 prisoners are incarcerated according to their security designation, minimum to maximum. Jimmy Lee has earned the right to be in the E-2 cell house, which accommodates two men to a room. Jimmy Lee's cell has a metal door and a window; there are no iron bars.

At six feet, four inches tall and nearly 300 pounds, Jimmy Lee is an imposing figure. His gentle and soft-spoken nature, however, offset his menacing size. He likes to keep to himself, particularly given the attitudes of the youthful offenders who fill the prisons these days.

"You can't say nothing to them," he explains. "I don't want to have to worry about always watching my back."

When Lipps had first met Jimmy Lee in 1982, he was impressed with his gentleness. "This is not a killer," he remembers thinking to himself.

Jimmy Lee's greatest pleasure comes when someone compliments his work; he is a part of the paint detail at Wilcox State Prison. He prides himself on the speed and professionalism he brings to the job, and hopes painting is a skill he will be able to use "on the outside." His free time, which he tries to minimize as much as possible, is spent listening to the radio and writing letters. He likes to make cards for his girlfriend, a woman who started writing to him when he was on Death Row years earlier. He also corresponds regularly with his siblings; both his parents died during his incarceration.

Even though Clemenstine cut all ties with him before he left the county jail, Jimmy Lee remains close to Ayoka. He and his stepdaughter continue to be involved in each other's lives despite the fact that Clemenstine now lives with Ayoka and her five-year-old daughter. Jimmy Lee also managed to maintain contact with his son, Rodney, over the years and became personally reacquainted with him in 1992, when Rodney was locked up on a drug charge. Jimmy Lee convinced the warden to put his son in his cell block, and the two men grew close during their joint incarceration. Jimmy Lee, of course, remained behind bars when Rodney was released, and it was there that he learned of his son's death in a drug-related incident in early 1997.

Jimmy Lee's constant nemesis is boredom. Each new day is a battle with loneliness and tedium. Sometimes the days seem unbearably empty, leaving him feeling particularly depressed. So he picks up a broom when he is bored, and writes a letter when he is lonely. He works hard to maintain a positive state of mind, and hold on to his hope of leaving.

"With my job, I feel like I'm contributing," he says. "I want my dormitory to be the cleanest one around, and I want the paint crew I work on to be recognized as the best of the best." His ultimate and overarching goal is to be free, but it is his work behind bars that keeps him going until then.

larry heath

In some ways, Shelby and Larry Heath's wedding on September 3, 1987, was not unlike the many other weddings that occurred that day. Like most brides and grooms, Larry and Shelby were completely in love with and committed to each other. That much was clear to Larry's parents, who had not been invited to either of Larry's previous weddings. And many other couples had no doubt begun their relationships by corresponding with each other, as Shelby and Larry did in June 1986. Surely they were not the first couple to get engaged only one month after first meeting each other. Nor was Larry the first groom to get down on one knee when he proposed to Shelby. He may not even have been the first to put his beloved's billfold on the floor before setting his knee on top of it so as to avoid getting his white pants dirty.

What was distinctive about both Larry's proposal and his wedding was that they took place in the visiting yard at the William C. Holman correctional facility in Atmore, Alabama. Larry wore white on both occasions because all inmates on Death Row at Holman are required to wear white. His marriage was the first performed at Holman in over fifteen years, and the first marriage of a Death Row inmate ever to take place in Alabama. Both the prison's warden and the state's Commissioner of Corrections had initially denied Larry and Shelby's request to marry, but the officials relented after the U.S. Supreme Court ruled in 1987 that all inmates have a fundamental right to marry.

Larry and Shelby each viewed the other as a miracle brought by God when one was needed most. Despite the obvious limitations on their marriage, not the least of which was never being able to consummate it, they both viewed their union as an extremely happy one. But less than four years after exchanging their vows, Larry and Shelby's marriage ended in the same place it began. On March 20, 1992, Larry was executed, leaving Shelby a widow.

Shelby was Larry's third wife. His first marriage, to Susan Taylor, was brief and ended in divorce. His second marriage, to Becky McGuire, lasted about three years. It ended in death, a death that Larry paid for with his own life eleven years later. On August 31, 1981, Becky McGuire Heath was kidnapped in Russell County, Alabama, and killed by a gunshot wound to the head. Her body was found in the backseat of her automobile off a county road in Troup County, Georgia. She was nine months pregnant at the time. She left behind a two-year-old son and a husband who was sentenced to death for having planned and paid for hers.

. . . .

When Larry married Becky in August 1978, at the age of twenty-seven, he felt that he had finally found someone with whom he could be happy. Larry even enjoyed spending time with his in-laws, with whom Becky was close. "What drew me to them," he later explained, "was the love I felt in their home. It was something which had been lacking in my life, leaving me with a void." He was delighted when Becky became pregnant and was instantly besotted with his son, Hamilton.

But as Larry's devotion to Hamilton grew, his relationship with his wife deteriorated. He began to have affairs with other women, frequent night-clubs, and stay away from home as much as possible. It was not only his marriage that suffered. He also lost interest in his work and ceased attending church

Larry later attributed much of his unhappiness to the fact that in July 1980, he came to believe that Becky was having an affair. He claimed that he confronted her about it and demanded a divorce and complete custody of Hamilton, but Becky refused because she did not want to tarnish the picture-perfect image her religious family had of her marriage.

From that point on, Larry slept on the couch or in his son's bed. His interaction with his wife consisted of heated arguments in which he demanded a divorce and she refused. His marriage was a sham, but he could not leave it because that would also mean leaving Hamilton. He was stuck.

In January 1981, Becky informed Larry that she was pregnant. Larry believed that the baby was not his, because he and Becky had not had sex since he had accused her in July of having an affair, six months before. Larry was furious. He had been assured by Becky that the affair was over. In his statement to the police on February 10, 1982, Larry described the impact the news of the pregnancy had on him.

> **So, I knew it wasn't mine. So I knew they were still seeing each other. There was proof enough of that. My reaction to this pregnancy was completely different from the first for the simple reason I knew it wasn't my baby. To describe the feelings I felt is hard for me to do now, but there was anger and there was hate. I thought that I had done everything that I should have and it was like everything was being thrown back in my face.**

"It's his baby, not mine, and I'm not going to support it," Larry told

Becky, and again requested a divorce. "So let me have Hamilton and you can have the other baby. It's yours," he said.

But Becky still would not consent. Larry toyed with the idea of simply leaving with Hamilton, but he didn't want to get in trouble with the law again. Prior to marrying Becky, he had spent a year in prison after using stolen credit cards that he had found, and he vowed he would never get locked up again. He had too much to lose.

To the outside world, Larry and Becky continued to have an idyllic marriage. They moved into a new home in Phenix City, Alabama, and Larry began working as a salesman for his father-in-law's business, Banner Buildings. But as Becky's abdomen grew with what Larry believed to be another man's baby, Larry found his home life more and more intolerable.

His unhappiness with his marriage was not the only reason Larry wanted out. In mid-May, he sold a camper top to Denise Lambert, a twenty-year-old horsewoman from Virginia who was spending the summer showing horses and staying as a guest of the commandant at nearby Fort Benning. The camper top was a special order, requiring a few return visits on Denise's part. By the time the sale was complete a few weeks later, Larry and Denise were dating.

Shortly after meeting Denise, Larry contacted his eldest brother, Ricky, and asked him if he knew anyone who would kill someone for money. Ricky initially told Larry he would help him out, but then never contacted him again. Larry next turned to his middle brother, Jerry. At the time, Jerry was "running the streets a fair amount," so Larry figured he would know the type of people who would do a contract killing. After bugging Jerry about it repeatedly, Larry was finally promised that his brother would look into it. Jerry told Larry there was a guy named Slim, from whom he purchased marijuana, whom he would ask.

By July, however, Larry was no further along. He began to feel desperate because he knew "the baby was fixing to be born" and that "with the baby's delivery, [he] would be trapped." He confronted Jerry at his workplace, at which point Jerry informed him that he didn't want to have anything else to do with it. Jerry had pieced together that it was Becky whom Larry wanted killed, and he wanted no part in helping with his sister-in-law's murder. By the end of the argument, however, Larry had convinced Jerry simply to tell him where Slim lived, and he would take it from there.

Larry finally tracked down Slim at the end of July. He showed Slim photographs of Becky and of her car, and agreed to meet later at Banner Buildings to come up with a plan. Slim showed up with two other men, who were introduced to Larry as Lumpkin and Cash. Larry walked off to the parking lot with Cash, who identified himself as the one who would do the killing, and gave him the photographs. All four men then batted around ideas for how to actually do the killing, but Larry did not like most of the other men's suggestions. They agreed to meet at Slim's apartment the next morning to finalize a plan. Larry also promised to loan Cash his .357 Magnum, since Cash, the hired killer, did not own a gun.

The next morning Larry handed over his gun, wrapped in one of Hamilton's diapers, and agreed to pay the men $2,000. Larry's understanding was that the gun would be used only to scare Becky, because he wanted her death to result from a car accident so that it would not look suspicious. He told Denise what he was up to, but justified his plan by making up a story about how Becky had cleared out all the money in his savings account, money that he had been saving for his new life with Denise. What Denise did not know, however, was that Larry was still married to Becky. She believed him when Larry told her that they had divorced, but that he was continuing to live with Becky for appearance's sake. Larry had already given Denise an engagement ring and had recently assisted her in arranging for the printing of wedding invitations. Denise was also unaware that Becky was nine months pregnant.

The murder was scheduled for the following day, but it did not actually occur until early August. The plan was called off on several occasions because Lumpkin's car wouldn't start, and then there was a mix-up with locating Becky. After the second failed attempt, Cash disappeared with Larry's gun and the four hundred dollars Larry had given him to have the car fixed.

In mid-August, Larry put the remaining sixteen hundred dollars in a plain white envelope and gave it to Denise for safekeeping. Then he met with Slim and Lumpkin again. They agreed that the best plan was to surprise Becky at home and then get her out of the house. Lumpkin pulled a .32 chrome-plated pistol out of his pocket and assured Larry, "We can take care of it."

Slim and Lumpkin were scheduled to surprise Becky between 7:00 and 8:00 A.M. the following morning, since she was planning to drive to her mother's house after breakfast. Larry met them just over the border in Georgia, then led them back to his home in Russell County, Alabama. He gave them the keys to his car and house and took off with Denise in her truck. Then he left Hamilton with Denise and went to work, arriving at Banner Buildings at about 8:45 A.M.

Larry repeatedly called Becky's mother throughout the morning to see if Becky had shown up, but her increasingly worried mother kept telling him that she hadn't arrived. At about 1:30 P.M. Slim showed up at Banner Buildings and told Larry that "it had been done." When Larry pressed him for details, Slim informed him that his partner, presumably Lumpkin, had shot her in the eye and that she was lying in the backseat of her car.

Larry was not pleased that Slim and Lumpkin had not adhered to the plan they had made together earlier. As he later told the detective who questioned him: "I asked him why in the hell that happened, cause she wasn't supposed to be shot. I've got enough sense to realize when you have got a violent crime you are going to bring in a ton of investigators, instead of an automobile accident and I knew then it was only a matter of time before yourself [referring to the detective] or somebody else picked me up."

Larry refused to turn over the rest of the money until he learned whether Lumpkin and Slim had left a lot of damaging evidence in their wake. As he explained in his statement: "Well, when they told me she had been shot I knew that things did not look good for me at all. That there was going to be a lot of suspicion as far as I was concerned 'cause of the manner it was done. And I told them, I said, 'You let me find out exactly what happened and I'll get back with you later.'"

Denise, however, was eager to make the payoff. Slim called her to demand the rest of the money he and Lumpkin were owed. Larry was several hours away at the time, staying with Becky's grandfather in Pine Mountain, Georgia, where Becky's funeral was held. When Larry called Denise, she told him that she felt she was being threatened and did not want to hold off paying Becky's killers. Larry reluctantly agreed to let her make the payoff so that Slim would stop harassing her.

Denise also conveyed how hurt she was to find out that Larry had been less than truthful with her. The newspaper accounts of Becky's death reported that Larry and Becky were still married. Denise went to the courthouse in Russell County to see if the divorce had been filed and learned that it was not even in the works. Larry also sensed that Becky's pregnancy, particularly given how far along it was, bothered Denise a lot. As he put it later, "Sometimes we don't realize what we have done 'til it's been done."

Larry spoke with Denise by phone the following night and confirmed that she had, in fact, given Slim the money. The next time he spoke with her, and the last time he saw her in person, was at the Georgia State Patrol Post.

. . . .

Rebecca McGuire Heath and Hayden, the baby she had been carrying, were buried side by side behind Oak Grove Congregational Christian Church. It was the same church where Becky and Larry had been married three years earlier. At the funeral, Larry seemed agitated and restless. Sandra McGuire, Becky's mother, tried to comfort her son-in-law.

"Don't you worry, Larry," she said, as reported in a three-part series about the murder in the *Columbus Ledger-Enquirer.* "Whoever killed Becky will be caught and punished." Little did she realize that her words were not comforting to her son-in-law.

"But you don't understand," Larry muttered. "You just don't understand."

Larry had spent the previous afternoon at West Georgia Medical Center awaiting the results of Becky's autopsy. He sat in the waiting room, with his elbows on his knees and his face buried in his hands. One of the Georgia Bureau of Investigation (GBI) agents noticed, however, that Larry peered at the agents through his fingers and followed them with his eyes. The agent had a gut feeling that Larry was only acting the part of the grieving husband.

That same day the Columbus police chief, Jim Wetherington, received a tip that Larry Heath had a girlfriend. GBI agents followed Denise Lambert for two days before finally confronting her, at which point she gave them enough information to justify questioning Larry.

Late on the afternoon of September 4, 1981, the Troup County sheriff, Gene Jones, called Larry at his in-laws' farm and informed him that the police were ready to release Becky's car, but that he wanted the entire family to go down to the patrol post to pick it up. When they arrived at the patrol post, Sheriff Jones and the Russell County sheriff, Prentiss Griffith, asked Larry to come with them. Larry handed Hamilton to his mother-in-law and followed the two men into another room.

Larry knew they were onto him. He had told Denise the night before that it was only a matter of time before he was considered a suspect. He had already been questioned about his gun, which he could no longer produce for them since Cash had disappeared with it. He was also aware that the circumstances of Becky's death were highly suspicious. It did not take long for GBI agent Bill Maleug, the chief investigator, to convince Larry that they had broken the case.

"We didn't have anything on him then," Maleug later told the *Columbus Ledger-Enquirer.* "When he opened up, he really surprised us by implicating all those other people that were involved."

Larry waived his *Miranda* rights and gave a full confession, admitting that he had arranged his wife's kidnapping and murder. On February 10, 1982, Larry pleaded guilty to the Georgia murder charge in exchange for a sentence of life imprisonment. By doing so, he was not only avoiding exposure to the death penalty, but would be eligible for parole after serving as few as seven years in prison.

· · · · · · · ·

In mid-October 1981, less than two months after Becky's murder, the McGuires were granted temporary custody of Hamilton. In November, Larry appealed the custody order, surprising everyone with the intensity of his opposition. In his mind, Becky's murder was rendered meaningless if he forfeited his parental rights, since the only reason he had not simply left Becky in the first place was so that he could maintain custody of Hamilton. His retained counsel, paid for by his parents, unearthed a Georgia law that stated that killing one's spouse did not automatically lead to forfeiture of parental rights.

On June 25, 1982, the McGuires were finally successful in terminating Larry's parental rights. In September 1983, two years after they were granted temporary custody of Hamilton, the McGuires signed the final adoption order.

· · · · · · · ·

Larry's parents had taken him a Bible soon after his arrest, but Larry wouldn't even touch it at first.

"I was too busy blaming God, and I was convinced that He had allowed everything to happen," he explained to Shelby. "I couldn't forgive myself, so I couldn't comprehend, nor understand how God could forgive me."

As painful as the custody battle was for Larry, he later pointed to it as the beginning of his religious salvation. As he put it:

> I was crushed; mentally, emotionally and physically drained. I had lost everything of any importance to me. But my son had meant more to me than life itself. It took that fatal blow from the court to make me get down on my knees in my cell and ask the Lord to come into my life and take it over completely. I repented and asked forgiveness for my sins. As I prayed that night for strength and peace of mind, God became very real to me.

Once he turned to the Bible, Larry underwent a change in his outlook and in his personality. Even though he was in a solitary cell at the time of his salvation, Larry no longer felt so alone. He found particular meaning in a verse of scripture in the book of Hebrews, chapter 13, verse 8, which states, "Jesus Christ, the same yesterday, and today and forever." To Larry this meant that, no matter what he had done in the past, Jesus still loved and wanted him. As he described it, "It was as if a tremendous weight or burden had been lifted from me and I began to view everything from a new perspective, in a different Light. His Light. I had a peace of mind which I had never known before. . . . It filled an emptiness and a void I had known all my life."

Larry's salvation did not come a moment too soon. Having suffered through the agony of permanently losing all ties to his beloved son, he was next confronted with his prosecution by the state of Alabama. Throughout his trial in Russell County, Alabama, Larry was able to remain "calm, passive, and unconcerned about the entire ordeal," even though a second conviction carried with it the threat of the death penalty. "A lot of people misinterpreted my lack of emotion for something else," he said. "But my peace and strength came from Jesus Christ and His promises to me. No matter what took place within that courtroom, they couldn't hurt me anymore."

On May 5, 1982, less than one month after Larry's guilty plea and life sentence in Georgia, the grand jury of Russell County, Alabama, returned an indictment against him for the capital offense of murder during a kidnapping. Despite Larry's objections, he was extradited to Russell County in the fall of 1982. Michael Raiford, the Phenix City attorney who represented Larry, and Larry Roney, a Russell County attorney, contested the indictment on two grounds. They argued that Alabama did not have jurisdiction over Larry's case, since the crime had occurred in Georgia, and that his conviction and sentence in Georgia barred his prosecution in Alabama for the same conduct.

Both claims were rejected by the trial court. It held that the Constitutional prohibition against double jeopardy did not bar successive prosecutions by two different states for the same act. The Russell County judge also ruled that Alabama had jurisdiction to prosecute Larry for the murder and kidnapping that had occurred in Georgia because the offense had actually commenced in Alabama.

The jury for Larry's trial was drawn from Russell County. Between the date of the crime, August 31, 1981, and the start of the trial on January 10, 1983, Russell County was saturated with pretrial publicity regarding all aspects of the case. It was reported in more than a hundred accounts that Larry Heath had pled guilty or was convicted and was serving a life sentence for the murder of his pregnant wife. There was also publicity regarding the McGuires' dissatisfaction with the life sentence Larry and his co-defendants received in Georgia, as well as details about the McGuires' custody battles.

Larry's defense counsel moved for a change of venue, asserting that "a large portion of the jurors have formed an opinion as to Defendant's guilt." The trial judge delayed ruling on the venue motion until after the completion of the voir dire examination of the jurors. Only twenty of the eighty-one jurors questioned had not heard of the guilt adjudications. Even those twenty, however, were apprised of Larry's guilty plea by the conclusion of voir dire because Larry's court-appointed attorney informed them of it when asking them about it. Nevertheless, the judge denied the request for a change of venue.

As Larry's subsequent petition to the U.S. Court of Appeals for the Eleventh Circuit put it:

> **Ten of the twelve jurors ultimately selected to decide the case knew, before they were even summoned for jury duty, that [Larry]'s guilt had been determined in Georgia. The other two learned of it from defense counsel in voir dire. As a result, all twelve jurors selected to hear the case knew that [Larry] had already pled guilty to the murder of his wife.**

It was U.S. Supreme Court Justice Thurgood Marshall who said it best, though, in his dissent to the 1985 decision affirming Larry's conviction. "With such a well-informed jury," he wrote, "the outcome of the trial was surely a foregone conclusion."

In January 1983, a jury in Russell County Circuit Court in Phenix City, Alabama, convicted Larry of capital murder. On February 10, 1983, one year to the day after he had been sentenced to life imprisonment in Georgia for the very same murder, Larry Heath was sentenced to death.

Four of his five codefendants were also subsequently prosecuted by Russell County, but all fared better than Larry. Slim Owens was originally convicted and sentenced to death, but his conviction was reversed because the prosecutor had used his peremptory challenges (in selecting the jury) in a racially discriminatory manner. Slim then entered a guilty plea and received a life sentence. Lumpkin was convicted and received a life sentence to be served concurrent to his Georgia sentence. Jerry Heath pled guilty to conspiracy and received a ten-year sentence. Denise Lambert negotiated a plea in both Alabama and Georgia, and she received a ten-year sentence in Alabama, to run concurrent with her Georgia sentence. She was released after serving thirty-three months. Charges against Sander (Cash) Williams were *nol prossed*, or essentially dropped, by Alabama authorities in exchange for his testimony. Of the six people who were charged and prosecuted for Becky's murder, including Slim and Lumpkin, who had done the actual killing, only Larry Heath ended up with a death sentence.

. . . .

Larry found some solace in the fact that he was able to "lead fellow Death Row inmates to Christ," and he became known as the "Apostle of Death Row." "Just as he served Satan 100 percent when he was in the world," Shelby later said of Larry, "he was now giving God 110 percent—all out, no holds barred." Indeed, it was Larry's religious fervor that Shelby initially found so attractive, and which served as the catalyst for their correspondence and subsequent relationship.

One night in April 1986, Shelby wrote a poem and mailed it to her nephew, David, who was also on Death Row at Holman prison. David showed Shelby's poem to Larry, who had been allowed out of his cell that day to do odd jobs on his tier, and asked him what he thought of it. Larry liked the poem and asked David to tell Shelby so, but David told him to tell her himself. Larry did just that, writing Shelby a one-page note and enclosing a copy of his personal testimony of what the Lord had done and was doing in his life. Shelby wrote back to him on June 1, 1986, at which point they began corresponding regularly. Larry called Shelby for the first time on July 1; she visited him for the first time on August 1; and he proposed to her on September 1, 1986. They were married a year later, on September 3, 1987.

Both Larry and Shelby felt that their love for each other was unconditional, which in turn helped them to understand and accept God's love for them. Both felt that it was the first time they could truly be themselves. As Larry put it,

> In the beginning, I made my life and the crime I was involved in an open book for her to examine. She accepted me as I am now, not as I once was. She was able to look beyond my past and see a future. After a deep struggle within and without for the both of us, we began to realize that our being together was part of God's plan in our lives. Love blossomed and grew.

Despite the many obstacles their physical separation presented, Larry and Shelby considered their marriage a blessing. They maintained daily contact through letters and spoke with each other as often as possible. Seeing each other was another matter. Shelby described their evolving routine:

> Visitation days for Death Row at Holman are Monday or Friday of each week. An inmate is allowed one visit per week. If he receives a visit on Monday, he cannot have another one on Friday. So, in order to see Larry, I had to take a day of vacation each visit. Visiting hours are 8:00 A.M. to 2:00 P.M. Atmore is approximately 220 miles from Birmingham, so in order to get there by 8:00 A.M., I had to get up at 3:00 A.M. and leave by 4:00 A.M. My employer was very understanding and considerate and allowed me to take my vacation a day at a time so that I was able to stretch it out so that I saw Larry an average of three times a month. Although his telephone privileges varied over the six years we were together, they finally stabilized and he was able to call me every four days. On the day that his tier got the telephone, he would call me twice—once in the morning before I went to work, and again at night when I got home. And we wrote each other every night.

. . . .

When Charlotta Norby first met Larry Heath, she did not sense any remorse on his part. She was usually able to focus on the legal issues of a case rather than the underlying crime, but Larry's was a particularly heinous one. She was also uncomfortable with the intensity of his religious conviction, since she neither shared nor understood his beliefs.

What emerged over subsequent visits and enabled Norby to respect and relate to Larry was his sense of humor. He was able to make light of even the most dire situations, and in a way that put everyone around him at ease. Norby was also impressed with Larry's refusal to feel sorry for himself. His positive outlook and demeanor were all the more striking when compared with other clients of hers who became increasingly bitter and vindictive as their execution dates neared. Larry wanted a reconciliation with the McGuires, but he also understood and appreciated their anger. He held nothing against the guards and prison administrators who were responsible for locking him up each day and accepted ultimate responsibility for his predicament.

And even though Norby was never able to relate to Larry's religious conviction, she did grow to appreciate its strength and sincerity. Larry's greatest virtue, however, was not revealed until the time of his execution. What Norby most admires about Larry to this day is the way in which he dealt with it. He never wavered in his religious conviction, and he never expressed any fear or weakness. His entire focus was on making his death easier for those around him. Indeed, Larry did not even want Norby to attend his execution, hoping to shield her from it. Instead, Norby was left wishing that she could have somehow done the same for him.

When Norby first received the case, joining Stephen Bright as co-counsel, she was hopeful about reducing his sentence. At the time, she was still relatively new at the Southern Center for Human Rights, having arrived there only months before receiving the case in the fall of 1989. She was not, however, new to criminal defense work; she had studied and worked in the field in various capacities for years.

When the Southern Center for Human Rights took over Larry's case, it was on appeal to the U.S. Court of Appeals for the Eleventh Circuit. The U.S. Supreme Court had already decreed in a 5 to 4 decision that Larry's conviction in Alabama did not violate his constitutional right to be free from double jeopardy. The Court decreed that the double jeopardy clause did not apply in Larry's case because he was prosecuted by separate jurisdictions.

With the highest court of the nation ruling against him, Larry began to despair. He considered dropping his appeals and forcing the state to execute him. In his testimonial, he wrote: "The decision was a bitter pill for me to swallow. So many attorneys and law professors were certain there would be a reversal by the high court, I was beginning to believe it myself."

Larry had been represented by volunteer lawyers in his appeal to the U.S. Supreme Court and in earlier, postconviction proceedings. He was furious because they had filed his federal habeas corpus petition, as well as a motion for summary judgment, without informing him or consulting with him. After learning that the U.S. District Court for the Middle District of Alabama had denied Larry's habeas corpus petition without a hearing and granted the state's motion for summary judgment, Larry wrote to U.S. District Court Judge Robert E. Varner on October 3, 1989, to express his dismay.

> **They were guilty of not addressing issues, dropping issues, and waiving issues. In addition, they failed to respond to specific instructions or orders from the court. From your court opinion, I also learned that my legal counsel had made major decisions without bothering to consult me. I am referring to the lack of response to the state's summary judgment motion and the filing of a motion for summary judgement on my behalf.**
>
> **I had no idea, or prior knowledge of their decisions, actions or inaction on my behalf. If I had been consulted, I would have made my objections and protestations known. I feel they bear the sole responsibility for the mishandling of my appeal.**

Given that many defendants are unable to find anyone to represent them for free in the appellate process, Larry was fortunate that the Southern Center for Human Rights (SCHR) was able to take over his case once he fired his first set of volunteer attorneys. The SCHR fully appreciated the urgency of his plea for help, since his case was very far along in the appellate process. Rendering Larry's predicament even more dire was the fact that Larry Roney, who was one of two attorneys who represented him at trial and had been appointed by the court to handle his direct appeal, had filed only a one-page brief. He had not even shown up for oral argument. As a result, many of the key issues in Larry's case were waived or barred because they had not been presented to the Alabama Supreme Court on direct appeal. Among the issues that the federal court could not examine as a result of Roney's shoddy representation was the trial judge's failure to grant a change of venue or excuse for cause the many jurors who knew about the Georgia guilty plea.

Norby's first order of business, upon receiving the case in the fall of 1989, was to collect all the case records and files. She was instantly struck by the amount of publicity there had been prior to Larry's trial, particularly given that much of the publicity mentioned his prior guilty plea. The fact that all twelve of the jurors who ultimately sentenced Larry to death knew he had already pled guilty to the crime before the trial even began was mind-boggling to Norby. Larry's case seemed to represent a clear violation of the double jeopardy clause, but the U.S. Supreme Court had already ruled against them on the issue.

Since the case was already on appeal to the U.S. Court of Appeals for the Eleventh Circuit, Norby knew that what she most needed to do was buy herself and Larry some time. On February 12, 1990, she filed a Motion for Relief from Judgment with the U.S. District Court for the Middle District of Alabama, essentially asking the district court to reopen its order granting the state's Motion for Summary Judgment. In a surprising move, the district court granted Norby's motion on April 30, 1990, allowing her to file an amended petition. Even though the district court ultimately denied the amended petition on July 24, 1990, the Eleventh Circuit had meanwhile dismissed Larry's initial appeal without prejudice. The end result was that Norby was able to include new issues in the amended appeal that had not been raised in the initial appeal.

· · · · · · · ·

Joan and Roscoe Heath live in the same house in Columbus, Georgia, in which they raised their three boys. It is a small ranch house filled with religious paintings and icons, such as the plaque that reads, "As for me and my house, we will serve the Lord." Many of the portraits of Jesus were painted by the Heaths' youngest son, Larry, while he was on Death Row at Holman prison.

Also lining the walls are framed certificates attesting to the fact that both Joan and Roscoe Heath are ordained ministers. They "turned their lives over to the Lord" in 1977, and were called to preach the following year. Their religious conversion occurred too late, however, to affect the childhoods of their sons. Larry's recollection of his religious upbringing, as reported in an interview with him in the *Gulf Coast Christian Magazine*, was that "[t]he only time we heard God in our house was profanity—followed by 'damn.'"

At the time of the murder and the trials, the media made much of Larry's childhood and the way in which he was raised. Roscoe and Joan felt unjustly accused. "They acted like it was all our fault," Joan complained, "even though Larry was an adult at the time."

Much was made in the press of the fact that Larry was totally estranged from his parents at the time of the murder, having excluded them from his marriage to Becky and the birth of their son, Hamilton. Joan Heath, hearing of her grandson's birth secondhand, tried to visit shortly after he was born, but Larry would have nothing to do with her. Even though it broke her heart, and she cried all the way home, she maintains with pride that Larry never saw her cry at the time. Both she and her husband expressed bewilderment at the way in which their youngest son divorced himself from them. Roscoe admits he was a domineering and aggressive father before he "found the Lord," but he maintains that Larry never needed much disciplining growing up because he was an "obedient boy."

Larry's recollection was that he and his father could not sit in the same room together without arguing. He attributed many of their disagreements to the fact that his father drank quite a bit, although Larry claimed he never saw him drunk. "He was a big man and consumed a lot," Larry told the *Gulf Coast Christian*. "Maybe he built up an immunity or something. I don't know."

In retrospect, Larry decided that his parents demonstrated love in the best way they could. But he did not feel they were a close or loving family. Larry was a shy and awkward boy with no self-confidence, and he attributed his insecurity to the frequent moves his family made when he was young. In high school, Larry came out of his shell. He played drums in the high school band and became gregarious and outgoing. With his new self-confidence, however, came a disdain for his parents. He perceived his mother as totally submissive to his domineering father, and he wanted nothing more to do with either one of them.

Since Larry's own religious conversion did not occur until after he was incarcerated, he was skeptical of the changes he perceived in his parents when he was in his early twenties. He couldn't accept their newfound commitment to God or what struck him as "another way to impress people." By the time he met and married Becky McGuire, he had severed all ties with Joan and Roscoe Heath.

When Joan and Roscoe were no longer in direct contact with Larry, they kept tabs on him through his brothers and other family acquaintances.

They knew that Larry was living beyond his means and was always in debt. As his father put it, their youngest son had "a Champagne appetite with a beer pocketbook." They did not know, however, that his relationship with Becky had soured or that he had turned to his brothers to help him have her killed.

When the Heaths attended Becky's funeral, having heard about her death from a nephew at church, Larry struck them as the bereaved widower. They tried to comfort him and hug him, but he would not even look at them. A few days later, however, Larry called them, sobbing. He was in LaGrange Prison by then, and he had already confessed to the crime. The Heaths, having learned of the importance of forgiveness from their own conversions, did not hesitate in offering Larry, as they put it, their "financial, spiritual, and emotional support."

Roscoe Heath immediately called an attorney friend of his in Columbus, who agreed to meet with Larry and assess his case. "I'm not going to take your money," he told Roscoe after learning of Larry's confession. "He has already condemned himself to death. It would eat up all your money, and for nothing."

The Heaths instead retained an attorney to fight the McGuires' efforts to terminate Larry's parental rights by suing for custodial rights. They knew it was a lost cause, but they wanted to do something tangible for their son. The custody battle ended up costing them far more than legal fees, since the McGuires' charges that the Heaths were unfit parents were printed in the local papers (the McGuires' attorney was able to dig up some embarrassing details of their preconversion life). The Heaths also suffered the pain and humiliation of having their middle son, Jerry, tried and convicted for conspiracy to commit their daughter-in-law's murder.

Even though Larry was taken from Roscoe and Joan in the sense that he was locked up and sentenced to death, it was his incarceration that brought them together. Their relationship flourished while he was behind bars. They visited every Sunday while he was in LaGrange, and every couple of months once he was transferred to Holman prison in Atmore, Alabama. They attended his wedding with Shelby, whom they describe as "a nice Christian girl," and proudly followed his religious conversion.

Larry and his parents also exchanged a flurry of letters and gifts. Joan Heath still chuckles about the time she sent Larry a Christmas package containing donuts and shampoo. By the time the package reached him, the shampoo had spilled out all over the donuts. Larry later told his mother that he and his friends blew bubbles with each bite of a donut.

Larry's offerings to his parents consisted of his artwork, most of which was religious, as well as contemplative letters and religious testimonials he wrote about turning to Christ. His mother's favorite card, however, is one she received long before Larry left home. It is a Mother's Day card he made for her when he was in elementary school. She re-reads it often, finding the words particularly prophetic, given the remainder of her son's life.

> **This old world we're livin in**
> **Is mighty hard to beat**
> **You get a thorn with every rose**
> **But ain't the roses sweet.**

. . . .

Norby believed that the oral argument before the Eleventh Circuit Court of Appeals had gone well, and she began to feel hopeful about the outcome of her client's case. It was the first time she thought they actually had a shot at getting Larry off of Death Row. The court's decision, however, instantly set her straight on how things stood. Instead of remanding the case for a new trial, the Eleventh Circuit affirmed the District Court's denial of habeas relief. Norby notified Larry:

August 28, 1991

Dear Larry,

Enclosed is a copy of the opinion from the Eleventh Circuit. I know you have talked to Steve and that the two of you will talk again later in the week. If there is anything I can do or anything you would like to talk to me about, be sure to let me know.

I am very very sorry that the court came out this way. It is always impossible to predict what will happen, but I must admit I was beginning to be very hopeful and that this was a shock and a great disappointment. I know you will not find it encouraging reading.

We will, of course, continue to do our very best and as you know there are still places we can [turn] to and things we can do. As we think about this and begin to figure out what to do, we will be in touch with you.

In the mean time, hang in there, and be sure to let us know if there is anything we can do.

> Sincerely,
> Charlotta Norby
> Attorney at Law

Norby and Bright immediately petitioned the U.S. Supreme Court for certiorari and were denied. They then began the laborious process of putting together a clemency petition, since their legal options for saving Larry were exhausted. Even though clemency petitions are last-ditch efforts with low success rates, Norby and Bright had some hope that Larry's request for clemency would be seriously considered. Alabama's governor, Guy Hunt, was a minister himself, so they thought he would be impressed by the large number of people who were convinced of the sincerity of Larry's religious beliefs. They arranged for the many ministers with whom Larry was affiliated to get involved, and they submitted the clemency petition in the ministers' names.

One of the ministers, Buford Lipscomb, the pastor of Liberty Church in Fairhope, Alabama, took an active role in trying to save Larry's life. Lipscomb first met Larry at the suggestion of another minister, Jim Britnell, who held church services on Death Row at Holman prison every Tuesday night. Britnell was so impressed with Larry's commitment to Jesus and the work he was doing on Death Row that he approached Lipscomb with the possibility of ordaining Larry as a minister. On February 27, 1992, Larry was ordained as a minister of the Liberty Fellowship of Churches and Ministers. The service was held at Holman prison and was attended by several ministers and Death Row inmates. The incident marked another historic "first" for Larry, since it was the first time a Death Row inmate was ordained while incarcerated.

Reverend Lipscomb met with Governor Hunt and told him about the impact Larry was having on others in the prison. He also met with the McGuires, in the hope that he could get them to support his request for clemency. Both meetings went well, leaving Lipscomb confident that Governor Hunt would commute Larry's sentence before an execution date could even be set. Lipscomb was wrong.

On February 10, 1992, the Supreme Court of Alabama issued the following order:

IT IS NOW ORDERED that Friday, March 20, 1992, be fixed as the date for the execution of the convict, Larry Gene Heath, who is now confined in the William C. Holman Unit of the Prison System at Atmore, Alabama.

IT IS, THEREFORE, ORDERED that the Warden of the William C. Holman Unit of the prison system at Atmore in Escambia County, Alabama, execute the order, judgment and sentence of law on March 20, 1992, in the William C. Holman Unit of the prison system, by causing a current of electricity of sufficient intensity to cause death to pass through the body of the convict, Larry Gene Heath, until he is dead; and in so doing, will follow the rules prescribed by law.

On Tuesday, March 17, 1992, Reverend Lipscomb presented Larry's clemency petition to Governor Hunt's legal counsel. The legal counsel assured Reverend Lipscomb that Governor Hunt would take the entire application for clemency home with him on Wednesday, read every letter written on Larry's behalf, pray over the situation, and reach a decision sometime on Thursday. That afternoon, Lipscomb issued a press statement:

Larry Gene Heath is scheduled to die in Alabama's Electric Chair this Friday. Larry has been known for a number of years as the "apostle of Death Row," a title given to him by his fellow prisoners. We have asked the governor to stop Larry's execution in favor of life without hope of parole.

This is an unusual movement, not only because pastors are coming forward from a wide number of denominations, but we're here representing those who are for and against the death penalty. . . .

Larry is guilty of murder, but this is not a case of jailhouse religion. Larry has had an enormous impact on his fellow death row inmates, and even some of the prison staff, over the last six years.

It is because of this impact that we believe society will be better served by allowing Larry to live. If Larry is granted life without parole, he will be placed in the general prison population. There will be a greater number of prisoners who will be significantly changed. Many of these will be short-term inmates. When they walk out those prison doors, because of the change in their lives, society will be safer.

Some of us have met with the victim's family. We do not want to minimize their grief or give any appearance of being insensitive to their pain. The McGuires are wonderful, Christian people.

In closing, let me state again, we feel that society will be better served if Larry is allowed to live and continue his tremendously effective ministry.

The clemency petition contained letters from eleven different ministers, all of whom attested to the sincerity of Larry's religious faith and his "positive and inspirational influence on fellow inmates and others."

The sincerity and intensity of Larry's faith is manifested through his interactions with and concern for others. Larry started and leads a daily group of death row prisoners who spend their exercise period in prayer. He has organized and leads a prayer chain of death row inmates. He helped teach a Vietnamese prisoner to read. He befriended a severely mentally disturbed prisoner. When several family members of a fellow prisoner were killed in an automobile accident after a visit to the prison, Larry helped initiate a letter writing campaign of support for the family. Larry has also written to members of other prisoners' families to help mend breaches in communication or relationships.

Everyone present at the meeting with Governor Hunt's legal counsel was optimistic about the outcome of the clemency hearing and so were Larry's supporters. As Shelby put it, "I knew beyond doubt that God's Hand was on Larry. I could not see how God could possibly allow him to die when He had poured so much knowledge, wisdom and ability into Larry." She recognized, as did Larry and the ministers and attorneys working on his behalf, that his crime should not go unpunished. They were not asking to have him set free, but rather to spare his life so that he could "spend the rest of his natural life in prison, [where] he will be punished more severely than any other participant in this crime, including the people who actually committed the murder, and more severely than scores of other Alabama prisoners who are serving life sentences for murder."

Early Tuesday evening, Governor Hunt announced on television that there would be no clemency for Larry. Even though the execution was not scheduled until one minute after midnight on Friday, March 20, 1992, leaving Governor Hunt with two more days to "carefully review and pray over" Larry's request for clemency, he denied it within hours of receiving it.

By the time Shelby reached Larry, he had already heard the news from Bright. When she asked him what he was doing, he responded, "I'm cleaning out my cell." That was the moment that "reality came crashing in" on Shelby.

> **I began to cry and to tell him I wasn't ready to let go of him. He was so strong for me, encouraged me to cry and reminded me that we probably wouldn't be alone again until the last two hours of visiting time from 8:30 to 10:30 Thursday night. A lot of friends and relatives were scheduled to come in on Wednesday and Thursday. So we talked and cried and even laughed until around midnight.**

Before receiving his own death sentence, Larry had been in favor of the death penalty. Shelby had also been a proponent of executions, even going so far as to say, "If their problem is that they can't find someone to pull the switch, call me—I'll do it." While their own conversions on the issue had occurred long before Larry's actual execution date approached, they both knew that Governor Hunt was responding to the public who had not yet been enlightened. As Larry put it, "[A] great philosopher once said that if we all lived by the words in the Old Testament, 'an eye for an eye and a tooth for a tooth,' we'd all be blind and toothless. He makes sense, you know, in the absurd."

. . . .

On Wednesday, March 18, 1992, Larry Heath was moved from his cell in Death Row to the "death cell" near the execution chamber. His cell had been cleaned and his belongings moved during visiting hours, depriving him of an opportunity to return to his tier and see his fellow inmates one final time. Larry was disturbed at the abruptness of his departure, but also relieved that he was spared the gut-wrenching task of saying good-bye to his friends.

Even though the guards continued to be friendly and accommodating by allowing for extended visiting hours during his final days and making other exceptions with respect to food and the number of visitors allowed, their interactions with Larry took on an almost comical degree of formality. For instance, they began to document his every word and move, including an instance that struck Shelby as particularly funny. As she recounted the story, "[Larry] said he was reading his Bible, lying on his back on the bunk, and he would doze off as he was reading and the Bible would fall on his face and wake him up. He said this happened several times, and the officers watching made a note of it every time."

Larry's final day was spent with his family and friends, as well as the prison's warden and minister. Larry refused his final meal so that he could spend more time with his visitors, since he would have had to be taken out of the visiting yard to eat it. At 7:30 P.M., Reverend Britnell led everyone in communion and then asked Larry if he had anything to say. Larry, visibly shaken, told everyone that the last ten years in prison had been the best years of his life, thanks to Jesus. He then addressed everyone individually, concluding with a tribute to his wife. He referred to Shelby as his "miracle from God" and praised her for the sacrifices she had endured by marrying a man on Death Row.

At 8:30 P.M., at Larry's request, everyone but Shelby was asked to leave so that Larry and Shelby could spend Larry's final two hours of allotted visiting time alone. They were not, of course, truly alone since the visiting yard consists of a glassed-in room with a hallway surrounding it on all sides. Several guards stood outside the windows, observing Larry's and Shelby's every move. They watched as Larry took off the Star of David necklace Shelby had given him for Christmas, slipped his wedding band on the chain, and then fastened the necklace around Shelby's neck. They watched while husband and wife cried together, calling out to God "to help us during this time of parting because we couldn't do this without Him." And they watched as Larry and Shelby hugged and kissed each other for the last time.

"Rest in Jesus," Shelby whispered.

Larry walked away from her, as he had done at the conclusion of all her previous visits, but this time he did not look back. Shelby knew she would never again see her husband alive, since he did not want her to attend the execution.

. . . .

Morris Thigpen dreaded executions. As Alabama's Commissioner of Corrections, he was responsible for overseeing the state's Department of Corrections and all of the prison wardens. Since the state required the warden of each prison actually to serve as the executioner by pulling the switch, Thigpen felt he, too, must attend. He hated doing so, however, which was a well-known fact in Alabama. Thigpen always stated in post-execution press briefings that he was "very much bothered" by that aspect of his job. He had attended five executions prior to Larry Heath's, one of which had to be carried out a second time because there had been a problem with the chair. It was Larry's, however, that took the biggest emotional toll on Thigpen.

Before Larry was strapped in the chair, he gave his Bible to Reverend Lipscomb, whom he had selected to attend as his minister.

"Give this to Shelby," Larry said. "I won't be needing it anymore."

Thigpen was impressed with how calm and fearless Larry appeared. He was shocked to find Larry's sense of humor still intact minutes before his death. After reading the execution order aloud, the warden asked Larry if he wanted to make a statement.

"How much time do I have?" Larry shot back, grinning.

Larry apologized for his crime and asked the McGuires for forgiveness. He also assured the warden and the guards who were present that he had only positive regard for them and did not hold them responsible for what was about to happen. He then turned to Thigpen and addressed him directly.

"Commissioner, I really wish that I could have gotten to know you better," Larry said. "I've heard a lot of good things about you." After a pause, he added, "You know, you should come down here more often. These folks on Death Row need to see more of you."

Thigpen was deeply touched. Here was a man whose life was about to be taken from him, and he was taking the time to tell the man ultimately responsible for his own execution that he would have liked to know him better. Thigpen had a hard time concentrating on Larry's subsequent comments, because he was struggling to hold back his tears. Larry asked the warden if he could pray, and then proceeded to do so. Thigpen knew without a doubt that this was a changed man; one could not fake such obvious devotion and belief. He was utterly awed by Larry's acceptance of his death and his "expression of love and understanding for what was about to take place."

"Lord, I'm coming home," Larry said, looking straight ahead.

They pulled the switch.

bar What members of the legal profession, particularly attorneys, are collectively called (as distinguished from the *bench*, which refers to judges). Each attorney is required to obtain bar admission in a particular state or court jurisdiction in order to be licensed to practice there. *Bar admission* requirements are satisfied by passing a bar examination (one part of which is a multistate exam that is universally applied to all states), and establishing a period of residency or by receiving reciprocity based on membership in another bar or jurisdiction.

certiorari A *writ of certiorari* is an order issued by an appellate court to a lower court when the higher court has discretion on whether to hear an appeal. If the writ is denied, the court refuses to hear the appeal and, in effect, the judgment below stands unchanged. If the writ is granted, then it has the effect ofordering the lower court to produce a certified record of a particular case tried below so that the higher court may inspect the proceedings to ascertain whether there were any irregularities. It is most commonly used to refer a case to the U.S. Supreme Court, which uses the writ of certiorari as a discretionary device to choose the cases it wishes to hear. A *cert. petition* refers to a request by an appealing party to have a higher court exercise its discretion to grant a writ of certiorari.

court-appointed attorney The Sixth Amendment to the U.S. Constitution provides, in part, that "in all criminal prosecutions, the accused shall enjoy the right . . . to have the Assistance of Counsel for his defense." In 1963, following the U.S. Supreme Court ruling in *Gideon v. Wainwright*, this right was made applicable to all the states. In addition to the local public defender's office, most states also rely on the appointment of individual attorneys to handle criminal cases. The fees and hour limitations are statutorily imposed and are significantly below those of the private bar. For instance, the court-appointed attorneys who handled Judy Haney's case in Alabama were paid twenty dollars per hour up to a limit of two thousand dollars for out-of-court time. There is often no additional training or experience required of court-appointed attorneys, beyond passage of the state bar, even for those assigned to capital cases, where the defendant's life is at stake.

deposition   A *discovery* device by which one party asks oral questions of the other party or of a witness of the other party. The deposition is conducted under oath outside of the courtroom, usually in one of the lawyers' offices, prior to trial. A *transcript* (word-for-word printed account) is made of the deposition, which can then be used at trial.

discovery   The pretrial devices that can be used by one party to obtain facts and information about the case from the other party in order to prepare for trial. Tools of discovery include depositions upon oral and written questions, written interrogatories, production of documents or objects, permission to enter upon land or other property, physical and mental examinations, and requests for admission.

double jeopardy   The constitutional (Fifth Amendment) prohibition against a second prosecution after a first trial for the same offense. In the context of the prohibition against double jeopardy, a court proceeding that may result in incarceration places a person in "jeopardy."

exculpatory evidence   Evidence that tends to justify, excuse, or clear the defendant from alleged fault or guilt. Following the 1963 U.S. Supreme Court case of *Brady v. Maryland*, the state is required to disclose all exculpatory material in its possession.

extradition   Most states have adopted the Uniform Criminal Extradition Act, which requires the surrender by one state of an individual accused or convicted of an offense outside its own territory and within the territorial jurisdiction of another.

habeas corpus   The name given to a variety of writs designed to bring a party before a court or judge. The primary function of the modern *writ of habeas corpus* is to release an accused from unlawful imprisonment. Initially, the writ permitted a prisoner to challenge a state conviction only on constitutional grounds that related to the jurisdiction of the state court. The scope of the inquiry was gradually expanded and now extends to all constitutional challenges. However, a criminal defendant can petition for a writ of habeas corpus only after he has been convicted and has exhausted his state appellate remedies.

hearsay   At a trial or hearing, a statement made by someone other than the declarant (the person testifying) during testimony that is offered in evidence to prove the truth of the matter asserted. Hearsay evidence is admitted only in specified cases by necessity, as outlined in one of the exceptions to the Hearsay Exclusionary Rule in the federal rules of evidence.

jury challenge In most jurisdictions, each side has the right to a certain number of *peremptory challenges* to jurors at the time of impanelling. In addition, a party has the right to challenge a juror by furnishing a satisfactory reason why he or she should not be seated, such as bias or knowledge of the case. Unlike a peremptory challenge, for which no reason need be given, the party challenging a juror for cause must satisfy the trial judge that her reasons are compelling.

jury trial A trial before a jury, as opposed to before a judge. The U.S. Supreme Court has held that the Fourteenth Amendment to the U.S. Constitution guarantees a right to jury trial in all state criminal cases that, were they to be tried in federal court, would come within the Fifth Amendment's guarantee. In subsequent cases, however, the Court ruled that the right to a jury trial did not mean a right to a twelve-person jury in noncapital cases.

mental capacity or competence The ability to understand the nature and consequences of the act in which a person is engaged and the business he or she is transacting.

***Miranda* rights** The right of a person in custody to be informed of his right to remain silent and to be warned that anything he says can and will be used against him in a court of law. This right stems from the 1966 case of *Miranda v. Arizona.*

mitigating evidence Evidence that does not constitute a justification or excuse of the offense in question, but that can be considered as extenuating or reducing the degree of moral culpability.

peremptory challenge The right to challenge a juror without assigning a reason for the challenge. In most jurisdictions, each party to an action, either civil or criminal, has a specified number of such challenges. After using all his peremptory challenges, he is required to furnish a reason for subsequent challenges. A *peremptory strike* is a juror who has been struck from the jury as a result of a peremptory challenge.

plea bargain A mutually satisfactory disposition of the case agreed upon by the prosecutor and the accused in a criminal case. It usually involves the defendant's pleading guilty to a lesser offense or to only one or some of the counts of a multicount indictment in return for a lighter sentence. All pleas are subject to court approval.

postconviction relief proceedings   Hearings and appeals following a defendant's conviction of crime and sentence of death.

prima facie case   In a criminal context, it is a case in which the state's evidence compels the conclusion of the defendant's guilt if the defendant produces no evidence to rebut it.

pro hac vice   When an attorney who is not licensed to practice law in a particular jurisdiction is given the right to do so in a specific case.

pro bono   Legal work or services done free of charge. In addition to individual agencies and practice groups whose cases are exclusively pro bono, such as the Southern Center for Human Rights, many for-profit law firms take on a certain number or types of cases on a pro bono basis.

probable cause hearing   A procedural step in the criminal process at which a judge or magistrate decides whether there is a reasonable ground for belief that the accused person committed the crime charged.

recusal   The act of disqualifying a judge, or a judge disqualifying herself, from a case because of bias or personal interest.

remand   When an appellate court sends a case back to the court from which it came for the purpose of having some further action taken on it there. For instance, when a prisoner is brought before a judge on *habeas corpus*, for the purpose of obtaining liberty, the judge hears the case, and either discharges the prisoner, remands the case, or lets the lower court's decision stand.

venireperson   A member of a pool of jurors. The jury that is ultimately impaneled is selected from the larger pool of venirepersons, or prospective jurors, who were summoned by a writ.

writ   An order issued from a court requiring the performance of a specified act, or giving authority to have it done, such as *writ of habeas corpus* or *writ of certiorari*.

The Southern Center for Human Rights challenges discrimination against poor and disadvantaged people facing the death penalty and unconstitutional conditions in prisons and jails in the South. The center receives no government funding and welcomes all donations. The address is 83 Poplar Street, N.W., Atlanta, GA 30303–2122.